Praise for *Retirement Income for Life*

"Fred Vettese's new book, *Retirement Income for Life*, seems destined to become the bible of any new or near retiree challenged with converting large RRSPs and other savings into reliable income."

—*Jonathan Chevreau reporting in* MoneySense *magazine*

"When I've been asked for resources to help retirees who are now drawing down their life savings, I used to be at a loss. No longer. Fred Vettese has taken this complex subject and brought it to life in this highly readable volume with clear writing, practical recommendations and an expert's knowledge of the issues. This will be a fantastic resource for our members, and indeed all Canadian seniors."

—*Wanda Morris, VP of Advocacy, CARP*

"Fred Vettese offers a timely and clear-eyed perspective on the challenges faced by many Canadian retirees and provides practical strategies to help those who have accumulated some wealth to make the most of their savings."

—*Barbara Shecter,* National Post

"Planning for how best to draw down your nest egg—the 'decumulation' phase—is a topic too often neglected by the retirement finance literature and by many advisors. Fred Vettese has written an important book that addresses this need. I especially recommend a close reading of his 'five enhancements' as potential ways to improve your drawdown strategy."

—*David Aston,* MoneySense Magazine

"The decumulation playbook, simply and convincingly explained for everyone. I follow it myself."

—*Don Ezra, aw~~~~~~~~~~~~ nt and co-author of*
The Retireme~~~~~~~~~~~~

RETIREMENT INCOME
FOR LIFE

RETIREMENT INCOME
FOR LIFE

GETTING MORE
WITHOUT SAVING MORE

FREDERICK VETTESE

MILNER &
ASSOCIATES INC
· EDITING · PUBLISHING · COMMUNICATIONS · CONSULTING ·

ISBN 978-1-988344-05-8

Production Credits
Editor and project manager: Karen Milner
Copy editor: Lindsay Humphreys
Interior design and typesetting: Adrian So, Adrian So Design
Cover design: Adrian So, Adrian So Design
Printer: Friesens

Published by Milner & Associates Inc.
www.milnerassociates.ca

Printed in Canada
10 9 8 7 6 5 4 3 2

To my father, Mario, whose legacy will live on for decades to come

CONTENTS

ILLUSTRATIONS

PREFACE

Drawing down one's savings in retirement is something very few retirees do well, even with the help of professional advisors. Some retirees outlive their money. An even greater number deliberately underspend for fear of outliving their money. And many retirees from both camps simply waste a substantial part of their wealth without knowing it. The waste is the result of employing inefficient drawdown strategies or spending more than necessary on investment fees.

There are a number of reasons for this sorry state of affairs. First, drawing an income from one's savings was not a mainstream issue until recently. Most of the retirement planning literature to date has focussed on the task of *accumulating* money rather than *decumulating* it. Even the latest robo-advisors are geared to helping people build their nest eggs, not spend them. With over one thousand Canadians turning 65 every day, however, the cultivation of good decumulation practices has suddenly become an urgent matter.

Second, it seems nobody wants to see retirees spending their savings; certainly not the financial advisor who takes a percentage of their assets each year. Nor do retirees' children, who fear that they will (a) receive no inheritance or (b) have to support their aged parents in their later years. As for the person who is most aggrieved at seeing wealth diminish—well, it's the retiree. A declining account balance makes one feel financially vulnerable and this becomes an ongoing source of existentialist angst. As I note in Chapter 11, drawing down personal assets in retirement is hard to do because it is a grim reminder not only of our dwindling influence in this life but also of our own mortality.

A third reason decumulation is so difficult is that some of the best decumulation strategies are the kind that only an academic or an actuary can love. If your goal is to draw the most income with the least possible risk, you may have to take actions that go against the grain to make it happen. While those actions will almost certainly provide you with more retirement income in lean times, the odds are you won't find them very appealing.

Smart decumulation can seem unappealing because retirees have conflicting goals. What they say they want (and maybe even think they want), is quite different from what they actually want. In professional surveys, retirees consistently say that their biggest fear in retirement (after failing health) is outliving their money. It stands to reason that they would, therefore, embrace any strategy that minimizes the chances of that happening—but they don't. Yes, they want to have enough money to last a lifetime, but they also want to preserve their savings for the reasons mentioned earlier. These two goals are not compatible and the latter tends to trump the former.

So I hope that you will read this book with an open mind. If you have significant savings (six figures at least), I have no doubt that the strategies described here will put you in a stronger position to cope with another financial meltdown such as the one we experienced in 2008. Even if the capital markets behave themselves in the years to come—and let's all hope they do—you can still look forward to more income with less anxiety.

Frederick Vettese
August 2017

PART I

SETTING THE STAGE

1

MAKING YOUR MONEY LAST

My first lesson in spending came at the age of four. I am told that I frequently took money out of my mother's purse to buy candy at the local convenience store. (How I got to the store on my own is another story.) Sometimes it would be just a nickel or a dime, but I wouldn't hesitate to grab a five-dollar bill if there was no loose change.

I didn't get away with it, though. My mother tells me that she or my dad would get a call from the store saying that little Freddie had come in to buy a 5-cent chocolate bar. They would tell the store owner to give me what I wanted and send me home.

My older brother, who was all of six at the time, cautioned that if I kept up my profligate ways, the family would run out of money. There is no evidence that I heeded his warning, which frankly sounded a little alarmist to me even then. Nevertheless, my parents eventually decided enough was enough and made their money less accessible. That put an end to my shopping expeditions.

There are two things I learned from the experience: First, it is easier to spend someone else's money rather than one's own, a privilege I have rarely been able to repeat since age four. Second, I needed a better strategy if I wanted my spending habits to be sustainable.

Unlike most of the retirement literature out there, this book is about spending rather than saving. I am assuming that you, the reader, have been saving for a long time and have maybe even retired. The very fact that you are reading this book likely means you have somehow managed to accumulate a significant amount.

You would think that finally being able to spend your accumulated wealth in retirement would be the easy part, kind of like scratching a long-endured itch. Unfortunately, that is not the case. Drawing down savings is something that very few retirees do well, even when they have the best of intentions.

Carl and Hanna Retire

Consider the case of Carl and Hanna, a responsible couple if ever there was one. We will get to know them better in later chapters, but for now, here is what you need to know.

Carl is 65 years old and Hanna is 62. Both are psychologically ready for retirement, though not without some trepidation. While the freedom from work is appealing, retirement presents perhaps the biggest financial challenge of their lives: figuring out the best way to turn their life savings into steady income. On the eve of retirement, they have amassed a grand total of $500,000 in an **RRSP** plus $50,000 in **TFSAs**. (By the way, the total happens to be a little more than four times their combined average annual pay.) They want to be able to enjoy life, and this will require loosening the purse strings. On the other hand, they worry about outliving their savings. While over half a million dollars in investable assets sounds like a lot, will it be enough?

RRSP stands for Registered Retirement Savings Plan. Contributions made to an RRSP are tax-deductible, and investment income earned is tax-sheltered. Income tax is payable only if an RRSP is cashed out.

Unlike an RRSP, contributions to a **Tax-Free Savings Account (TFSA)** are not tax-deductible. They are nevertheless attractive because the investment income as well as any withdrawals are never subject to income tax.

In preparation for retirement, Carl and Hanna eliminated the mortgage on their home. In addition, they had been in the habit of paying off their credit card debt at the end of each month and making fairly regular contributions to their RRSPs.

Their next step is to visit an advisor at their local bank branch. There, Carl and Hanna learn that if they want to turn their $500,000 in RRSP assets into regular income, the money has to be transferred into a **RRIF** first. So they set up a RRIF account. (If their savings had accumulated in a pension plan rather than in RRSPs, the monies would have been transferred to a **LIF** instead.) They also talk to family, friends and other people who seem to be knowledgeable about investments. Their aim is to find a prudent and commonly accepted strategy for drawing down their savings.

RRIF (pronounced "riff") stands for Registered Retirement Income Fund. This is the vehicle to which RRSP monies are transferred in order to draw a regular, periodic income. The rollover from an RRSP into a RRIF is tax-free. It usually happens at the point of retirement but must take place no later than the end of the year in which one turns age 71. Withdrawals are subject to income tax. See Appendix B for more details.

LIF (pronounced "liff") stands for life income fund. It is much like a RRIF, but with a few extra restrictions. See Appendix B for more.

Here is a brief summary of what Carl and Hanna are told in the course of their investigation:

- It is best to invest their RRIF assets in well-known mutual funds,

- They should draw an income equal to 4 percent of their RRIF assets in the first year of retirement,

- Their income needs in future years will increase at the same rate as inflation so the drawdown from the RRIF should increase in lockstep,

- **Annuities** are best avoided, especially in a low-interest rate environment, and

- **CPP** and **OAS** pensions should be started immediately upon retirement—in this case at age 65 for Carl and at age 62 for Hanna—in order to extract the greatest value from government pension sources if they die early.

An (immediate life) annuity is a contract in which you give the insurance company a lump sum (like $100,000), which is called a single premium. In return, they pay you a fixed monthly or semi-annual amount for the rest of your life.

CPP means the Canada Pension Plan (or its Quebec counterpart, the QPP) and **OAS** means Old Age Security pension.

Let's get one thing out of the way before going any further. I could keep on using the term "drawdown," but I prefer the term **decumulation** instead. It suggests a certain symmetry because it is the opposite of "accumulation," which is what you were doing for most of your working life.

Decumulation is the process of drawing down one's financial assets after retirement with the primary goal of producing a regular income, usually for the rest of one's life.

The decumulation strategy described above is known as the 4-percent rule. Notice you do not draw down 4 percent of assets every year under this "rule," just in the first year. In future years, the amount withdrawn increases with inflation.

The mutual funds that Carl and Hanna choose, by the way, are from a big-name investment company with a reasonably good track record. They put about 50 percent in **equity funds** and the other 50 percent in a fixed income (bond) fund. The annual fee is 180 **basis points**, which is not low, nor is it especially high in the world of actively managed funds in the retail market. Because the fees are quietly deducted from their portfolio, paying them is relatively painless.

Consider **equities** to be another word for stocks. Owning the stock of a given company essentially gives you a share in the ownership of that company. When you put your money into an **equity fund**, you essentially hold shares in many different companies. Such diversification lessens your risk, but you will still experience gains or losses over any given period.

A **basis point** is 1/100th of one percentage point. For example, an annual investment management fee of 180 basis points on a $100,000 investment means you pay $1,800 a year (1.80 percent of $100,000).

When Carl and Hanna describe their decumulation strategy to their friends, everyone nods in approval. It would seem that the new retirees have done everything right and that financial security should be all but assured.

Unfortunately for them, the capital markets do not co-operate. The investments in their RRIF and TFSA perform poorly for a number of years following retirement. Markets will do this from time to time. In this case, the long bull market for stocks had finally run its course. After falling sharply from all-time highs, stocks then languish in the doldrums for a prolonged period. This is similar to what happened in the 1970s in North America. It happened again in the United States in the 2000s. Japan has been mired in this state since the early 1990s.

The fixed income portion of their portfolio does not do well either. That is because interest rates slowly climb for several years after their retirement. While it sounds like a good thing, rising interest rates create capital losses on longer-term bonds.

To compound their monetary misery, Carl and Hanna incur some unexpected expenses. Three years into retirement, they have to replace their roof, which comes with a $15,000 price tag. Five years later, their son, Arnie, runs into financial trouble. He had bought a bigger house but then lost his job and couldn't make the mortgage payments for a few months. Like the good parents they are, Carl and Hanna stepped in to help. They dipped into their RRIF to give Arnie the $12,000 he needed until he got back on his feet. Had they known their own investments would continue to do so poorly, they might have thought twice about it. But then again, how do you say no to a child in trouble?

At age 78, Carl undergoes a surgical procedure that restricts his activities for six months. The out-of-pocket expenses that Carl and Hanna incur, including hiring caregivers for a few months, set them back another $11,000. Actually, they shelled out $20,000 for these services but cut back on other discretionary spending to the tune of $9,000 while Carl was recovering.

In spite of the investment losses and the unexpected expenses, Carl and Hanna gamely stick to the spending regimen dictated by the 4-percent rule. The result, however, is not pretty. They exhaust their RRIF and TFSA assets by the time Carl is 82 and Hanna is 79, which leaves them with only their CPP and OAS pensions. The sad demise of their RRIF and TFSA income is depicted graphically in Figure 1.1.

Figure 1.1: Their Money Runs Out by Age 82

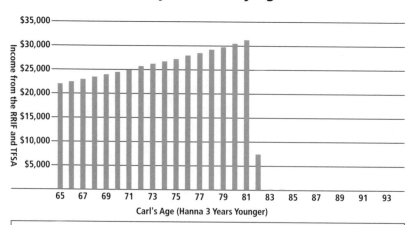

Carl and Hanna draw income from their RRIF and TFSA based on the 4% rule except they draw more income at ages 68, 73 and 78 to cope with spending shocks (not shown here). They had very poor investment returns.

How can this unfortunate couple do everything "by the book" and still end up living in near-poverty? If we are looking for culprits, there are some obvious candidates.

For instance, we might be inclined to chalk it up to bad luck given what happened to their investments. You might think no one is to blame and the result cannot be helped. The former conclusion may be true, but not the latter. We will find that our couple could have coped quite well in spite of their investment losses.

Another possibility is that the three spending shocks that Carl and Hanna incurred in retirement are responsible for derailing their retirement security. This is not true either. The frequency of these kinds of events and the amounts involved were not unusual. They should have been expected.

A third interpretation is that Carl and Hanna lived too long, but this possibility is ridiculous. Only actuaries think of living a long time as being an adverse result.

Finally, some people might conclude that $550,000 in savings was simply not enough for Carl and Hanna to provide the income they wanted and weather the usual risks. Even this is not true. They could have had twice as much, or even ten times as much, and if they followed the 4-percent rule to the letter, that money would still have run out by the time Carl was 82. The 4-percent rules simply does not work at any level of wealth if one experiences the type of poor investment returns that befell Carl and Hanna.

So, is using the 4-percent rule the crux of their problem? It's certainly part of the problem, but there are many other ways in which Carl and Hanna went wrong. For instance, they should have taken their other sources of income into account when deciding how much to withdraw from their savings. These other sources can vary year-by-year. Figure 1.2 shows total retirement income for Carl and Hanna.

Figure 1.2: Total Retirement Income for Carl and Hanna

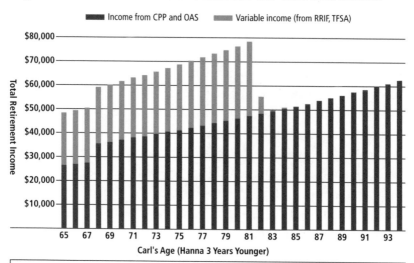

This is the same as Figure 1.1 except it includes income from CPP and OAS. Income jumps when Carl turns 68 because that is when Hanna turns 65 and starts to receive OAS pension.

Second, if they think their income needs will rise by the inflation rate, they should think again. Eighty-year-olds spend very differently than 60-year-olds do, so we should expect that their income needs will change at a different pace.

Third, Carl and Hanna shouldn't focus only on the income they will produce. The more important number is the amount of income they have available to spend, and this will depend on how much they pay in income tax.

These are just some of the issues that Carl and Hanna should have been considering; there are others.

It doesn't have to be like this. As we shall see in later chapters, much of what passes for conventional wisdom in the decumulation arena is just plain wrong.

We will find that Carl and Hanna could have started out with the same $550,000 in assets, encountered the same poor investment luck and still maintained a comfortable standard of living for the rest of their lives.

The first step, though, is to understand better what type of retirees they are and, by extension, what kind of retiree you are or will be. Understanding your own attitude toward money will dictate the best sort of decumulation strategy to follow in your particular situation.

Takeaways

1. Decumulation is not as straightforward as you might think; by comparison, the accumulation phase is child's play.

2. Disaster can strike even if you save a great deal, wait until 65 to retire and follow a widely accepted decumulation strategy.

3. The good news is that a bad outcome can be averted with a better decumulation strategy (which will be rolled out in the following chapters).

2

WHAT TYPE OF RETIREE ARE YOU?

There are a lot of things you could put on your wish list once you've retired, like DIY projects around the home, escaping winter in Florida or enhancing your culinary skills. Even though these activities sound totally unrelated, they all have something in common: they fall under the heading of **regular spending**. In that sense, they are the same as paying the food bill or buying car insurance. Regular spending would also include child-related expenses if grown-up children are still on your "payroll" after retirement. (Unfortunately, that is becoming more common in this era of boomerang children. Just remember your kids don't like it any more than you do.)

If you had to worry only about regular spending, then a one-size-fits-all decumulation strategy might work. Two other spending buckets also compete for your precious savings, though. One of them I call **"rainy day" spending** and the other is **bequests**. The priority you place on each of the three spending buckets defines the type of retiree you are.

Regular spending (bucket number 1) consists of all reasonably predictable and repeatable expenses such as food, tobacco and alcohol; routine home maintenance; hobbies; travel; utilities and insurance. These expenses will tend to be similar from one year to the next, though some are purely discretionary.

Rainy day spending (bucket number 2) involves expenses that you cannot easily anticipate and cannot ignore when they arise. They include big-ticket items such as major medical or dental expenses, an urgent request for money from a grown-up child or major home repairs.

Bequests (bucket number 3) are gifts of property by will; that is, the amounts you pass on to specific individuals or institutions when you die.

I see four basic types of retirees. Type 1 is the **mainstream retiree**, who held down a job, bought a home, raised children and paid taxes. (As Anthony Quinn declared in *Zorba the Greek*, "Wife, children, house, everything. The full catastrophe.") At the high end of the income scale, Type 1s are professionals, executives and successful entrepreneurs. The less affluent Type 1s also had steady jobs for the most part and earned a reasonably comfortable living. What they all have in common is a desire to maintain their lifestyle after retirement and avoid nasty surprises. While Type 1 retirees would not mind a financial windfall, they won't take big risks to make it happen. They don't worry too much about rainy day spending because the only spending shocks they can imagine are those they can absorb with a year or two of belt-tightening following the shock. Finally, Type 1 retirees are not prepared to reduce their spending much, if at all, in order to make room for bequests. That is what the equity in the house is for. By the way, Carl and Hanna are Type 1 retirees.

I call Type 2 retirees **the Cleavers**, not the butcher knife variety but rather the TV family from the iconic *Leave It to Beaver* show of the 1950s. Ward and June Cleaver would have been mainstream retirees were it not for the "Beaver" (son Theodore). The Beaver got in trouble in virtually every episode as a result of exhibiting consistently poor judgment. A real-life Beaver would find it difficult making his way through life on his own, which is why parents like the Cleavers figure they will need to continue providing financial support for their children, possibly even beyond the grave. Anecdotal evidence suggests that the Cleavers are a surprisingly common retiree type. I have many friends and acquaintances around retirement age who are quietly making provisions for a grown-up child who, they fear, might not otherwise be able to cope.

Type 3 retirees are the **super-savers**, people who could never bring themselves to spend lavishly. They regularly socked away a little more for retirement than they thought they would need, "just in case." Academics used to put this behaviour down to memories of the Great Depression, but Type 3s still exist. In their working lives, they would have behaved much like mainstream retirees, only with more saving and less spending. In retirement, the same pattern will most likely continue. They are almost certain to end up with a significant amount of unspent capital when they die. Of course, there is a chance that their retirement security could still be jeopardized by a variety of rainy day situations.

Then there are the Type 4 retirees, whom I label the **YOLO**s, as in "you only live once." YOLOs will want to spend more extravagantly in their early retirement years, even if it dims their longer-term prospects. Some people favour immediate gratification and so they are YOLOs by nature. Others become YOLOs because they think their life expectancy is shorter than normal and want to enjoy life while they can. Still others can expect a normal lifespan, but they buy into the notion that disability-free life expectancy is apt to be fairly short. (They might have gotten that idea from my last book.) YOLOs do not want to be destitute in old age, but their bigger fear is ending up with a great deal of unspent wealth. In my experience, YOLOs in Canada are rare. This is a little strange, as their philosophy seems perfectly rational, provided they exercise at least a modicum of spending restraint.

Sometimes, one type will blend into another. For example, the Cleavers will save more than average and will be difficult to distinguish from super-savers. Both save more than average, just for different reasons. Still, there are some differences in the priorities they place on each spending bucket.

The relative importance of each spending bucket varies by retirement type. I have tried to summarize the relationship in Table 2.1.

Table 2.1: Relative Importance of Each Spending Bucket, by Retirement Type

	Bucket 1: Regular	Bucket 2: Rainy Day	Bucket 3: Bequests
Type 1: Mainstream	High	Low to Medium	Declines over time
Type 2: Cleavers	Medium	Medium	High
Type 3: Super-Savers	High	High	Depends
Type 4: YOLOs	High	Low	Low

The reader might note that I have left out low-income households in my description of retiree types. By low income, I mean people in the bottom 30 percent of the income scale. This is not because their needs are less important but because they have much less need of a decumulation strategy than their higher-income counterparts. Most, if not all, of their income comes from defined-benefit sources like OAS, CPP and other government programs. In fact, most of them can expect to receive more after-tax income after age 65 than they ever enjoyed when they were still working, even if they never saved a penny.

And where does the worrywart fit into my scheme? You might think that retirees who worry a lot about their financial situation might be a separate type; but in reality, I have witnessed a spectrum of worry within each of the four types above. Some people will fret more than others by nature, whether they have reason to do so or not. My late father had accumulated considerable wealth in his lifetime thanks to some shrewd investments in real estate back in the 1960s, and yet he still had lingering concerns in his late 80s that his money would run out. Nothing could have been further from the truth, though. He lived very frugally to the end and my best guess is that he would have had enough money to last him and my mother until about age 300. To be sure, he was an extreme case. My father would definitely have been a super-saver. Perhaps he rests easier knowing his grandchildren will benefit from the legacy that his super-saving made possible.

Most anxiety in retirement, in fact, stems from the unpredictability of one's income stream, not the absolute level of income. If you had low but certain income, you might be miserable (or not) but you wouldn't be particularly anxious. Surveys show that retirees whose retirement income is variable (because they are living off their savings) are more likely to remain in a state of anxiety long after they retire. This response is totally rational. To a large extent, that is why I wrote this book—to offer an alternative decumulation strategy that will wring out much of the variability and lessen anxiety.

Perhaps the luckiest retirees from a financial perspective are those who have ample pensions from **defined benefit (DB) pension plans**. They tend to worry less about finances in retirement and spend more freely. Unfortunately, DB plans are dying out (except in the public sector) because of the financial strain they place on employers. Fewer than 10 percent of all workers in the private sector are still members of DB plans and this percentage will keep dwindling, as most DB plans are now closed to new members.

Defined benefit (DB) pension plans are workplace arrangements that provide a predictable amount of pension that does not depend on investment results or how long one lives.

The most important result that comes from a smart decumulation strategy is the ability to produce a stream of income that is stable and predictable, almost as if it came from a DB plan.

Takeaways

1. Spending in retirement falls into three categories or "buckets": regular spending, rainy day spending and bequests.

2. There are at least four types of retirees; the type of retiree you are dictates the priority you place on each spending bucket.

3. It is wise to know your retirement type before you formulate a decumulation strategy.

4. A good decumulation strategy maximizes the portion of your income that is stable and predictable. This is a sure-fire way of allaying your financial anxiety after retirement.

3

YOUR INCOME TARGET IN YEAR ONE

How much income will you need in retirement? It has to be enough to satisfy your regular spending as well as the other two spending buckets described in Chapter 2. I assume you don't want to drop your standard of living and you might even want to improve it a little. Whatever amount of income enables you to do that and still leave you with enough money to fill the other two spending buckets could be considered your **retirement income target**.

Retirement income target means the gross annual retirement income you need in your first full year of retirement. It is expressed as a percentage of your final average employment earnings, whereby the averaging is done over the last five years of work or perhaps over the last 10 or 15 years. There is no set rule for choice of denominator.

You might be wondering, why bother quantifying your retirement income target, especially if you are on the verge of retirement? By that time, your spending is what it is and if you haven't saved enough to generate the retirement income to fund it, then you'll simply have to spend less. Surveys suggest this is what most retirees tend to do anyway.

In spite of that, there are two good reasons why you should know your target. If you have not yet retired, it will help you to put your mind at ease. You may find your income target isn't as daunting as you thought. Or, if you do have to ramp up your saving, you'll have a better idea by how much.

If you are retired, having an income target can still be useful. Your spending can otherwise start to stray, either rising to a level that is not sustainable or falling lower than necessary. A target introduces some discipline to your financial habits in retirement, and it may even provide some reassurance.

Why 70 Percent May Be High

The traditional advice for middle- and high-income earners is to shoot for a retirement income target of 70 percent of final average earnings. Carl and Hanna earned a combined $120,000 a year in their final working years, so 70 percent translates into a target annual retirement income of $84,000. That sounds like more than they can possibly generate from $550,000 in savings, and it is. Fortunately, their real target is lower.

To the uninitiated, 70 percent might seem low, if anything. Why isn't it 100 percent? All you need to do is take a closer look at your paycheque to know the answer to that. Many items that whittled down your gross salary while you were working are no longer required. For example, you no longer need to contend with payroll deductions and work-related expenses. And for most homeowners, the mortgage is also usually paid off by retirement. Even the income tax payable in retirement tends to shrink as a percentage of income. And, of course, you don't have to save for retirement when you *are* retired!

Consider the comments by a real life–retiree, David Davidson, as they appeared in Rob Carrick's column in the *Globe and Mail* on August 4, 2017. Davidson observes:

> *You don't need as much money as the financial industry says you*
> *do. Sure, more money is better than less, but we sacrificed a lot*
> *to max out our RRSPs every year and then also max out TFSAs*

when they came along. I see now that we needn't have sacrificed so much while working. In fact, I find we have more money to spend in retirement than we had when we were working. Not having to furiously save for retirement frees up a lot of cash.

The real target for most people is lower than 70 percent (in some cases, a lot lower). In my past writing, I have explained the various reasons why this is the case, and it's nice to know I'm not alone in saying this.* A recent Canadian study shows that the vast majority of those from middle-income households who retired with enough income to replace 65 to 75 percent of their final average earnings end up with a much *higher* standard of living in retirement. An astounding four households out of five in this category improved their living standard by 20 percent or more. In some cases, the amount they had available to spend doubled! You will find these people in the lightly shaded area in Figure 3.1. In this chart, a Living Standards Replacement Rate (LSRR)** is synonymous with net replacement rate. An LSRR of 100 percent means you can maintain the same standard of living after retirement as you did before.[1]

Figure 3.1: People Who Retired with 65% to 75%

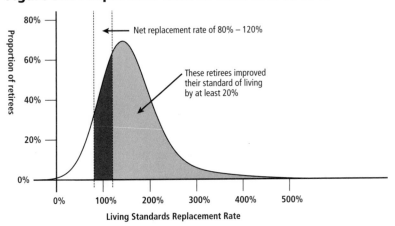

* For the record, I'm not even the first one to say it. Malcolm Hamilton has been expounding on this theme since the 1990s.

** Many thanks to Bonnie-Jeanne MacDonald, who not only coined the term Living Standards Replacement Rate but also gave me permission to use the chart in this book.

What makes this study so significant (and to my mind, credible) is that it was not commissioned by a taxpayer coalition or a right-wing think tank with an axe to grind. The authors were academics who simply followed the data.

If your employer enrolled you in a defined benefit pension plan that generates a replacement rate in the 70-percent range, then count yourself lucky. You can put this book down and go work on your golf game or your gardenias. If you need to generate income from your own savings, however, the good news is that you don't have to stress out if such a lofty target proves to be unattainable; it is probably not your real target.

The Real Target
If the retirement income target is not 70 percent, then what is it? As we will see, it can be almost anything you want it to be. To illustrate, I will compute a retirement income target for Carl and Hanna.

What we already know about our worthy couple is that both spouses worked right up until 65, accumulated savings in RRSPs of $500,000 plus another $50,000 in TFSAs and had final average pay (combined) of $120,000. We can now add some more details to complete the picture:

- Their two children were grown up and weaning themselves off the family payroll by the time Carl and Hanna were within six years of retirement; the children were totally self-supporting two years later.

- Thanks to lower child-related expenses, Carl and Hanna started to save a lot more in those last six years.

- Once they had paid off their mortgage (when Carl was 61), they had even more disposable income.

- They had the usual work-related expenses as well as CPP and EI deductions right up until the day they retired.

This is all captured in Figure 3.2, which is admittedly a little busy. The main message is that various types of expenditures can greatly reduce the income that working-age people have available for regular spending. The black portion of each bar in the chart indicates the amount that is available to them for regular spending, after deducting all their other expenses.

Figure 3.2: Breaking Down the Typical Paycheque

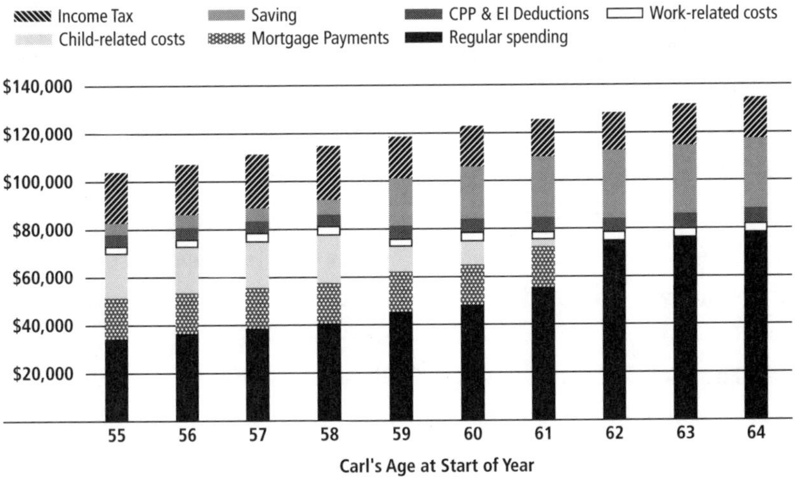

Carl's Age at Start of Year

Let's take away the noise now and focus only on regular spending. Just how much income do Carl and Hanna need to maintain their regular spending after retirement?

I figured this out in steps, starting with deleting all the other spending items shown in Figure 3.2 except regular spending. Then I expressed regular spending as a percentage of gross income instead of showing it in dollar terms. Finally, I grossed up those percentages to reflect the income tax Carl and Hanna will have to pay in retirement. The result of this exercise is shown in Figure 3.3. We now have a basis for determining their retirement income target.

Figure 3.3: Regular Spending (Grossed Up for Income Tax)

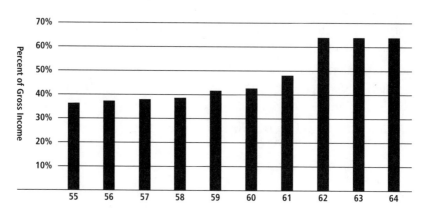

Two conclusions should jump out from Figure 3.3. The first is that regular spending as a percentage of gross income was quite low in some years. Responsible people who pay their taxes and meet all their other obligations live off a surprisingly small percentage of their gross income. Carl and Hanna were spending a mere 36 percent of their combined gross income on themselves at age 55.*

The second conclusion is that the amount of money available for regular spending (or saving) can jump dramatically once mortgage payments and child-related expenses drop off. Consider, for example, that the last three years in both of these charts are mortgage-free, and so the average amount available for regular spending is 64 percent, which is almost double what it was at age 55.

A 64-percent spending rate is almost certain to be unsustainable over the rest of their lives unless Carl or Hanna comes into a big in-heritance. They would need a lot more savings to make such a high target work. Fair enough, you might say, but what if they had saved enough money in the years leading up to retirement to support a spending rate of 64 percent? Well, they could have done that (may-be), but saving a lot more means having even less income left over to spend. As a result, they would never have experienced anything

---

* In fact, it would be only 33% if I hadn't grossed up the number for income tax payable.

close to a 64-percent spending rate during their working years. Can you see the Catch-22? Even some pension experts who should know better seem to gloss over it.

How then should Carl and Hanna set their target? Let's agree it is inappropriate to cherry-pick and consider only the three years of their lives when their capacity to spend was by far the highest. It is equally inappropriate to pick the lowest three years in the last 10. Perhaps they should base their target on the entire 10 years instead. After all, spending habits tend to change slowly, so the longer averaging period is a better predictor of spending habits that they might carry into retirement.

The average percentage of income available for regular spending over their final 10 years of work was 47 percent. This may seem modest compared to 64 percent, but it still represents a level of consumption that Carl and Hanna never enjoyed at any time before they reached age 60.

To summarize, Carl and Hanna will have some leeway in setting their retirement income target. It's nice to have a higher income, of course, but one has to be realistic. If Carl and Hanna set their income target at 47 percent*—and then round it up to 50 percent just to have a little cushion—they should feel content in the knowledge that they will be spending more on themselves in retirement than they ever did in their working lives (except maybe for the last three years). All we have to do now is find a way to make that 50-percent spending rate sustainable.

Drawing a Line in the Sand

It is one thing to set an income target and quite another to attain it. Keep in mind that income from savings can vary from year to year depending on market conditions. So besides setting their ideal retirement income target, Carl and Hanna should also define a lower income threshold, sort of like drawing a line in the sand. This lower

---

* Grossed up to reflect income tax payable. They actually spent closer to 43 percent in those final 10 years.

threshold would be the amount they can still live on without too much discomfort if they just don't have the assets to generate the retirement income they want. In this case, the lower income threshold will be less than 50 percent but perhaps not *that* much less. In going through their budget, they might conclude their total income could be as low as 40 percent of their working income without giving up too many of the things they love.

In the following chapters, we will assume that Carl and Hanna have set their upper income target at 50 percent and their lower income threshold at 40 percent. I will call the gap between 40 percent and 50 percent their "acceptable zone."

Takeaways

1. If you saved regularly, raised children and made mortgage payments, your retirement income target is unlikely to be as high as 70 percent of final pay, or even 60 percent.

2. You should know your own retirement income target. It helps you to calibrate your withdrawal rate after retirement. Before retirement, that knowledge should reduce your anxiety about your state of retirement-readiness.

3. You may have a few golden years before retiring when you are free of mortgage payments and child-raising costs. Before you hurry out to spend the extra cash, figure out your retirement income target and make sure you save enough to reach it.

4. The higher you set your retirement income target, the more you need to save while you're working and, therefore, the less you can spend before you retire. You need to strike a balance.

4

YOUR RETIREMENT INCOME TARGET IN FUTURE YEARS

Inflation may no longer be the terrible force it once was, but memories of past inflationary periods are still fresh enough to make anyone on a fixed income a little uneasy. It seems almost obvious that your income in retirement has to keep up with inflation.

Alas, what seems obvious isn't always true. While most goods do rise with inflation, your particular basket of goods is constantly changing as you get older. By the time you reach age 80, the contents of that basket will bear little resemblance to what it was when you were 60, much less 40. It would, therefore, be sheer coincidence if the cost of living rose at exactly the same rate for 80-year-olds as it does for younger people. The spending needs of retirees will tend to rise either more quickly or more slowly than general inflation. But which one is it?

As it turns out, most retirees eventually spend less in real terms once they reach a certain age. The difference in spending from one year to the next may be small, but it makes a significant difference over time.

What is amazing is that this finding should come as a surprise to anyone. I sort of knew about this phenomenon when I was 20. I received cash gifts every so often from my grandmother even though she had only a modest income (a small government pension from Italy). As it happens, her spending needs were even more modest.

I'm not the only one who knew something was going on, of course. In his 1977 book on the state of retirement in Canada, Geoffrey Calvert observed that "as age advances, clothing and footwear expenditures fall steadily to less than one half … furniture costs fall to one third … automobile-related costs to one sixth, while travel costs as a whole drop to less than one quarter."[1]

Calvert went on to say, "Even though the incomes recorded in this sample become significantly less as age advances, the ability to make gifts, add to assets and purchase discretionary and luxury items, seems to be surprisingly well sustained. One does not see reflected here a picture of increasing hardship as age advances."

If Calvert's remarks were true in 1977, they should carry even more weight today. Since the 1970s, Canada's seniors have grown steadily more affluent. Calvert's observations, however, have been all but forgotten. Most of us still think that our pensions need to increase each year with inflation.

Just because we choose to ignore a phenomenon doesn't mean it no longer exists. The data still suggest that older people spend less. It is hard otherwise to fathom how they could be saving such large amounts. According to CIBC, the elderly in Canada will be handing over a mind-blowing $750 billion to the next generation over the next 10 years alone![2]

If we fail to acknowledge the true spending patterns of older retirees, political correctness may have something to do with it. The mere suggestion that older people don't need quite as much money can come across as senior-bashing. But while it is a sensitive subject, I don't think it justifies our shying away from the truth. We would be doing a disservice to the retirees themselves, as well as to those planning for their retirement, by perpetuating myths. If younger retirees know what's in store for them, they can recalibrate their spending intentions now to reflect that reality. In other words, they can spend more now, knowing they will be spending less (in real terms) later on. Knowing this should make them feel less anxious about their future financial prospects.

I mentioned to a friend of mine a while back that older people spend less, and he immediately objected. He said his widowed dad (who was in his mid-80s) spent all kinds of money. I said, "Really? On what, may I ask?" He opened his mouth to tell me but stopped himself. He suddenly realized that most of his dad's extra spending was not on himself but on others. For instance, his dad was paying the rent for one of his daughters. His personal expenses were modest, as he seldom went out and no longer travelled.

Academic Studies on Retirement Spending

If there is any lingering doubt that seniors start spending less in **real** terms, then numerous academic studies from a variety of developed countries should dispel it. These studies, based on extensive data, make a compelling case that the drop in spending at older ages is a widespread phenomenon in developed countries. The tipping point for the slowdown in spending seems to occur in one's early 70s and then persists well into one's 80s.

Real spending refers to the level of spending after it has been adjusted for inflation. If inflation and spending both rise by 2 percent a year, one would say that real spending remains constant.

Here are some of the key findings from those studies:

In 1992, Axel Börsch-Supan studied the saving and consumption patterns of the "very old" (his words, not mine) in Germany.[3] By observing 40,000 households, he found that retirees tended to maintain their spending in real terms during their 60s. This result was expected. What surprised him was what happened around age 70. Instead of retirees continuing to draw down their savings, their assets started to climb again. Börsch-Supan

*determined that this happened because older German retirees
spent less in real terms. Eighty-year-olds were saving more than
45-year-olds! After testing all the possible reasons for the decline
in spending, he concluded that the reduced spending stemmed
from two causes. The first was a reduced ability to spend due
to creeping infirmity. If you can no longer get on a plane, your
travelling expenses decline, for one thing. The other cause was a
diminished inclination to spend. After the death of a loved one,
for instance, exotic travel might seem less interesting.*

*Actuary Malcolm Hamilton produced a landmark study in 2001
that showed that seniors in Canada save enormous amounts of
money.[4] Senior couples aged 75 and over either saved or gave
away as cash gifts an average of 16.1 percent of their income.
Couples 85 and older saved or gave away even more. Saving so
much indicated that super-seniors must be spending less. More
important, it also showed that the drop in spending had little
to do with insufficient income. The only plausible conclusion is
that the elderly are either not inclined or not able to spend as
much as they used to. Hamilton's finding is especially compelling given that the study encompassed seniors at all income
levels, not just the wealthy. The average income for couples 85
and over, for instance, was just $31,300. While Hamilton used
data from the late 1990s, his findings should be just as valid today given that modern-day seniors are much better off. Incomes
among seniors have risen nearly 20 percent in real terms since
the mid-1990s.*

*David Domeij and Magnus Johannesson reported that Swedes
also spend less as they age. Their 2006 study tried to explain
why.[5] The explanation that best fit the data was that failing
health made spending both more difficult and less enjoyable.
This was essentially the same conclusion as Börsch-Supan's.*

A 2015 UK study (Brancati et al.) sifted through two very large data sets: the Living Costs and Food Survey, and the English Longitudinal Study of Ageing.[6] They uncovered a precipitous drop in spending between ages 60 and 80. In spite of it, most of the 80-year-old respondents said that their spending was not constrained by a lack of money. The reductions in spending occurred at all income levels, by the way. Similar to the Börsch-Supan work, the tipping point for a slowdown in spending occurred around ages 70 to 74. As the authors noted, this is also when time spent at home alone starts to rise rapidly.

You might be wondering why I have not cited any Canadian studies other than Malcolm Hamilton's which is now nearly 20 years old. It is because good Canadian studies are hard to find. One possible reason for this, as mentioned earlier, is political correctness, a force from which even academics are not immune. A more tangible reason is that **longitudinal data** on consumption does not exist yet in Canada.

Longitudinal data refers to data gathered from observing the same subjects over a long period of time.

McKinsey & Company Canada did their best to overcome this deficiency using data from Statistics Canada's Survey of Household Spending.[7] They showed that spending drops sharply with age. Not everyone accepts this finding, however, as it was not based on longitudinal data and was not corrected for changes in household size. These apparent shortcomings do not mean the McKinsey findings were wrong; it's just that longitudinal data would be so much more compelling. For now, we have to rely heavily on the results from Germany, Sweden and the UK. The studies from these countries are hard to ignore. The data we do have for Canada makes it hard to argue that Canadians are fundamentally different.

Here are some metrics that help to pinpoint how fast spending declines:

A 2012 EBRI study by Michael Hurd and Susann Rohwedder concluded that real (inflation-adjusted) spending by college-educated married couples fell by 1.23 percent a year in their late 60s, 1.75 percent a year in their 70s and 2.75 percent a year in their early 80s.*

Another study from the United States, this one by David Blanchett of Morningstar, estimated that real spending declined by about 1 percent a year in the first 10 years of retirement, 2 percent a year in the next 10 years and 1 percent a year thereafter.

A third US study, produced by J.P. Morgan using its own data, found that real spending among affluent households dropped by 1 percent a year for the first 20 years of retirement.

The 2006 Swedish study mentioned above calculated a drop in consumption of 25 percent between ages 60 and 80.

The UK (Brancati) study reported that a household headed by an 80-year-old spends 43 percent less on average than a household headed by a 50-year-old. If one includes mortgage payments in the calculation, then 80-year-olds spend 56 percent less. The researchers used this and similar data to estimate that household expenditure in retirement fell by 1.4 percent a year. This is after having made adjustments for various factors such as household size.

---

* The Employee Benefit Research Institute (EBRI) is a Washington-based think tank.

Incidentally, all of the above studies (except for the McKinsey study) made adjustments for changes in household size over time. The usual reasons that households get smaller are because of children leaving the family home or the death of a spouse.

When it comes to the impact of household size, by the way, there is a broad consensus in academic circles that spending in a household is proportional to the square root of the number of persons in the household. Hence, the cost for two people is about 1.4 times the cost for one. The death of a spouse should therefore result in a reduction in household spending of about 30 percent.

Setting an Income Target for Future Years

Taking all the foregoing studies into account, I believe it is safe to conclude that the spending of seniors in real terms keeps up with inflation until age 70 or so, and after that it will usually fall at the rate of:

- 1 percent a year throughout one's 70s,

- 2 percent a year in one's 80s,* and

- 0 percent from age 90 and on.

There would also be a one-time drop of 30 percent or so when a spouse dies. When we factor these percentages into future spending needs, we can see how the retirement income target for Carl and Hanna changes over time. In the previous chapter, I had the couple choose an income target of 50 percent of their final average pay. If they follow the above spending pattern, their income needs should rise in line with inflation until about age 70 then rise more slowly throughout their 70s and rise more slowly again in their 80s. Spending would fall by a further 30 percent when Carl dies. This is all captured in Figure 4.1.

---

* Note that these percentages are slightly different from those used in my book, *The Essential Retirement Guide*. This reflects increased conservatism and the inclusion of data from a wider set of studies.

**Figure 4.1: Carl and Hanna's Retirement Income
          Target in Future Years**

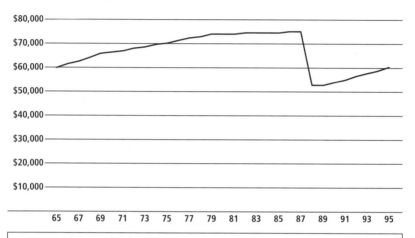

Income needs rise with inflation until age 70 but rise more slowly between ages 70 and 90.
When Carl dies at 88, Hanna's income needs drop by 30%. Assume inflation is 2.2% a year.

The Lower-Income Threshold

In Chapter 3, I identified two income targets for Carl and Hanna: their
ideal level of annual income and a lower threshold that represents the
amount that they could live with if circumstances dictated. Figure 4.1
shows the upper target at all ages. Carl and Hanna also established a
lower income threshold of 40 percent, which is the amount of spending they absolutely need if they want to avoid any real hardship. Their
acceptable zone for total income is between the lower and upper targets. This is represented by the shaded ribbon in Figure 4.2. Income
above that ribbon would be welcome of course, but consider that a
"nice to have" rather than a "must have."

Aligning Income Targets and Retirement Types

The retiree types were defined in a previous chapter. The acceptable
zone shown in Figure 4.2 as a "ribbon" is typical of what Type 1
(mainstream) retirees would aim for. Type 2 retirees (the Cleavers)
might have to settle for a lower income range so they can accommo-
date the future needs of an ageing Beaver. Alternatively, they save

more in their working years to attain this kind of target range. Type 3, the super-savers, would do the same. Finally, Type 4 retirees (the YOLOs) would raise the entire range for the first 10 or so years and then settle for a lower range for the remainder of their lives.

Figure 4.2: The Acceptable Range of Retirement Income for Carl and Hanna

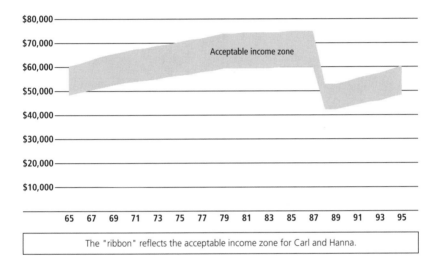

The "ribbon" reflects the acceptable income zone for Carl and Hanna.

The Income Targets and Government Benefits

For middle-income couples like Carl and Hanna, a sizeable portion of their overall income will come from CPP and OAS. The pensions from these two government programs are fully indexed to inflation so they will become an ever-increasing share of total retirement income over time. As a result, the income that Carl and Hanna generate from their savings does not have to be fully indexed to inflation. If inflation stays low (as I expect it will), that part of their income probably does not have to be indexed at all. This is good news because indexed annuities are hard to buy and it takes a lot more money up front to produce an increasing stream of income throughout retirement than it does to produce a flat amount. (I will have more to say about annuities in Part II.)

Of course, we're not done yet. We still need to decide how much money, if any, should be set aside for rainy day situations and bequests. These are the subjects of the next two chapters.

Takeaways

1. The amount of retirement income you need tends to rise more slowly than inflation, especially between ages 70 and 90.

2. You want to determine your ideal retirement income target as well as the lowest level of income that you would be prepared to accept. You also want to know how these income levels will change in the later stages of retirement.

3. The income that you generate from your savings does not need to be fully indexed to inflation.

4. The acceptable income zone can be a little higher or a little lower depending on the type of retiree you are.

5

RAINY DAY SPENDING

I used to think it strange that retirees would bother saving any money at all. Stranger yet is the fact that many of them save as much as they do. What is all that saving for?

As pointed out in the last chapter, much of the saving happens later on in retired life and it happens by default. Many older retirees are not able to get around as easily as they used to and, as a result, they spend less money. In addition, they may have lost a spouse or their enthusiasm wanes for other reasons and so spending on travel or entertainment no longer holds the same attraction.

Some of the saving might also stem from concern that they might outlive their money, but that cannot be the main reason. If it were, people would do most of their saving early in retirement when they face the greatest uncertainty and then gradually save less as their ultimate fate becomes more evident. This, however, is not the typical saving pattern in retirement.

There is at least one more reason for so much saving: fear of the unknown. As Mary Schmich says, "The real troubles in your life are apt to be things that never crossed your worried mind—the kind that

blindsides you at 4 p.m. on some idle Tuesday."* People understandably want to have the means to cope with the unexpected, especially
when they are living on a fixed income. We saw this with Carl and
Hanna in Chapter 1. They faced three significant rainy day events
in the first 15 years of their retirement, which is close to the typical
number faced by retirees.

The question is, how do you prepare for that "rainy day" in a way
that makes sense? This can be quite a challenge because the goal itself is so vague. Fortunately, the Society of Actuaries (SOA) can shed
some light on this problem. In 2015, the SOA investigated the type of
rainy day situations that retired Americans actually encounter and
how they cope with them.[1] I will focus on the survey respondents
with higher incomes and account balances, as these are the ones who
are more in need of a decumulation strategy.

This is not the first time the SOA has conducted surveys of retirees and pre-retirees. What was special about the 2015 survey is
that it marks the first time they focused specifically on older retirees.
The real-life experiences of people who have been retired for 10 or 15
years provide insights that you cannot get from that of their younger
counterparts.

Types of Spending Shocks
The SOA report listed the various spending shocks that retirees reported. When I looked at the list, the shocks seemed to fall into two
major categories: "supply shocks" and "demand shocks."

The supply shocks all involve a sudden loss of assets and the
belt-tightening actions that must follow from them. Using the wording from the report, the supply shocks included:

- a drop in home value of 25 percent or more,

- running out of assets,

---

* "Wear Sunscreen" was a hypothetical commencement speech by columnist Mary Schmich
  originally published in the *Chicago Tribune* in June 1997. Baz Luhrmann made it famous in
  1999.

- a loss in the total value of savings of 10 percent or more due to poor investment decisions or bad investment,

- bankruptcy, and

- loss of a home through foreclosure.

Notice that the supply shocks all relate to investment risk in some way. While these situations can be devastating, rather than discuss them here, it is better to deal with them in Chapter 7, which focuses on investment risks.

The demand shocks are different because they affect spending. You might have been getting by comfortably with only your regular spending to worry about when you suddenly get hit with a large and unexpected bill. The reason for that bill is almost always one of the shocks listed in Table 5.1. The table also shows how often these shocks occur according to the SOA's findings.

Table 5.1: Demand-Side Shocks in Retirement

Shock	Frequency
Major home repairs or upgrades	35%
Major dental expenses	26%
Significant out-of-pocket medical or prescription expenses	8%
A family emergency	6%
Victimization by a fraud or scam	4%
Significant damage to the home due to a fire or natural disaster	2%
Divorce during retirement	2%

Copyright © 2016 by the Society of Actuaries, Schaumburg, Illinois. Reprinted with permission.

In reviewing Table 5.1, three observations come to mind. First and foremost, the financial impact is really not that large for the most part. Consider major home repairs, for example. These repairs could include things like re-shingling the roof or replacing the furnace, which could cost several thousand dollars. While a bill of this size is unwelcome, it doesn't arise that often. And it is not so great that retired couples like Carl and Hanna cannot recover from it.

Home *upgrades,* as opposed to repairs, can cost a lot more but they are less frightening than repairs for the simple reason that you can opt not to make them. Strictly speaking, the expense of an upgrade is not even a shock because you can see it coming. It's not like you walk into your kitchen one morning and discover workers setting up scaffolding.

Hence, the second observation is that most of the events on the list are not even shocks in the true sense of the word. Even most home repairs should not come as shocks. Roofs and furnaces last only so long and therefore homeowners should not be surprised when they eventually have to be replaced. The oxymoron "foreseeable shock" comes to mind.

Moving on to major dental work, the cost is once again going to be in the thousands. This might cause you to delay or cancel some discretionary spending—like your next holiday—but it is not going to bankrupt a well-heeled retired couple.

As for medical situations, the chances that the cost will be catastrophic are exceedingly slim in this country because our universal health care system covers most of the big-ticket items. One study shows that health care expenditures of Canadian households at the 90th percentile are about $4,000 a year.[2] This means that nine times out of ten, such expenditures will be less than $4,000. Now, $4,000 is an inconvenience, but it is not going to lead to financial ruin for a couple that is otherwise well prepared for retirement. Besides, you have to assume that anyone who is spending this much on health care has had to curtail other activities. If so, then total spending rises by less than the cost of the health care expenditures.

About the only really expensive health care expenditure that might not be covered are certain new drugs that can cost $1,000 a month or more. There is some real exposure here, though fortunately the need does not arise very often.

If the retiree insists on going out of the country for medical treatment (especially to the United States), then yes, the bills can quickly lead to financial ruin. This is a matter over which the individual has control, however, and it is seldom done voluntarily except by the especially affluent. If medical treatment is needed while travelling out of country, well, there is no excuse for not having insurance.

Then there is the matter of significant damage to, or loss of, a home. The emotional shock is real, of course, and some items of sentimental value can be lost, but it should not result in significant financial loss; this is what home insurance is for.

My third observation is that the spending shocks that tend to be the most costly are the ones that involve other family members. Divorce after retirement is one of those events. It is not so much the legal costs that set you back, but rather it's the fact that your assets drop in half while your living expenses drop by only 30 percent or so. I confess I have no solution for this potential turn of events other than to over-save if you feel it is a real risk.

The crises of other family members can also cost you money. One common situation will be a grown-up son or daughter coming to you with an urgent need for money—due to business loss or job loss, for example—and needing financial help. If you feel it is your role to be your adult children's financial backstop well into your retirement when your own resources are limited, it is not my place to tell you differently. Just be prepared to deal with the consequences. I know of retirees who have taken out large mortgages on their homes to help out a son or daughter, even though they have no way of repaying the amount.

Ability to Cope with Shocks

You might be thinking that I am being a little casual in the way I'm brushing off the impact of the various demand shocks, so I will let the retirees speak for themselves. When asked in the SOA survey about their ability to manage within new constraints (following a shock), 93 percent of the retirees in the top third of the income scale said they managed "very well" or "somewhat well." Carl and Hanna would be in this top third. As for the middle third of retirees, 85 percent said they managed "very well" or "somewhat well."

My guess is that if the same survey was conducted in Canada, an even higher percentage of retirees would say they were managing very well. Not only are Canadians better savers and more prudent spenders (at least that is my impression), we have the **Guaranteed Income Supplement (GIS)** as a backstop. In addition, our so-called "socialized medicine" is less likely to result in a major bill to the patient.

Guaranteed Income Supplement (GIS) is a monthly non-taxable income benefit that is provided to Canadians with limited means after age 65. The amount payable is income-tested. If you and your spouse are receiving OAS pension, the GIS cuts out when income is above $23,184 (2017 level).

Setting Up a Reserve

So what do we do with this information? It appears that the vast majority of retirees muddle through reasonably well, in spite of the odd retirement shock. I would therefore suggest we don't try to overthink the matter of rainy day spending by devising too elaborate a strategy. As we will see, there are other, more serious challenges when it comes to decumulation such as coping with investment and longevity risk.

Most retirees would no doubt manage even better if they held a little money in reserve.

Carl and Hanna initially set their retirement income target at 47 percent, which I bumped up to 50 percent. It may have looked like I was merely rounding up but, in fact, Carl and Hanna are earmarking that extra 3 percent as money to be added to their rainy day reserve on a regular basis. That amounts to $3,600 a year at age 65 and increases in future years as their income target grows.

Toronto financial planner Rona Birenbaum confirms that the types of rainy day situations mentioned above do not faze her clientele. Some of them do set up a formal reserve for rainy day spending while others simply keep a large float in their chequing accounts.

My suggestion is to hold back a smallish percentage of your retirement income each year and use it to build a reserve for rainy day situations. This reserve may not totally cover all the shocks you might encounter, but it will definitely soften the impact. It would certainly place you among the better-prepared retirees. I admit that a reserve may not appeal to Type 4 retirees (the YOLOs), but other retirees should seriously consider it.

If you do set up a reserve, I would strongly suggest using the money only for rainy day situations. To avoid the temptation of treating it as mad money, you might want to keep it separate from other assets. In the case of Carl and Hanna, they ignored the advice to set up a reserve, until they hit their first spending shock at age 68. After that, they listened and were able to use the reserve to meet the spending shocks that came five and ten years later.

Long-Term Care Situations

The SOA survey did not consider long-term care as a rainy day situation. Long-term care is a complicated issue that deserves more space than there is room for here.* Let me say, though, that it tends to be a real financial problem for only a small fraction of the population. The majority of people will never need long-term care, and many of those who do will need it only for a relatively short period of time, like one or two years.

As for the rest, the very affluent can handle the costs as they arise. Those of modest means will have to rely on subsidized community-based care. It is only the people in the middle income group who need to make some hard decisions. Those with substantial equity in their homes might choose a more expensive option, such as home care with outside caregivers.

---

* I addressed it at some length in my book *The Essential Retirement Guide: A Contrarian's Perspective.* Of course, though, that is hardly the final word on the subject.

Takeaways

1. The financial shocks you are most likely to encounter in retirement tend to be small enough to be manageable.

2. The really big shocks tend to be events involving family members, like divorce or bailing out a grown-up child. The incidence of these types of shocks tends to be low or, in the case of helping children, within your control.

3. Hold back about 3 to 5 percent of your retirement income each year and keep it in a separate account to be used exclusively for rainy day spending.

6

PLANNING AN INHERITANCE

A little while ago, I had a call from Hugh, an old friend of mine from school. Hugh had undergone major surgery the previous year and, while it was successful, his insurance company informed him that his life insurance premiums would more than double to about $500 a month. Hugh was understandably distressed by the news and hoped I could give him some advice.

I started by asking him why he had the insurance in the first place. From where I sat, I couldn't see the need for it. Hugh was about 60 and could look forward to a generous and secure pension from the government after a career in the civil service. If he died, his wife, Beth, would receive 60 percent of that pension for life. She would also receive a substantial pension of her own from another public-sector pension plan. With all that pension income and a paid-off house, Beth would be better off financially without Hugh around. (She might also be better off climatically, as Hugh always kept the house too cold.) In any event, Beth clearly didn't need the life insurance proceeds.

Hugh and Beth also had a grown-up son, Ethan. This detail might seem irrelevant, as the life insurance proceeds would have gone to Beth, not Ethan. What is relevant is that Ethan stood to inherit the house as well as the death benefits from both of his parents' pension plans in the unlikely event they both died in an accident. He would be one rich young man without ever seeing a penny of the insurance money. The fact is, no one in that household really needed the life insurance. It looked like Hugh could save himself $500 a month.

By the way, you might be interested in Hugh's answer as to why he was trying to buy life insurance in the first place: "Isn't that what you're supposed to do?"

Even though the story above involves life insurance proceeds, it can apply equally to bequests. (The phrase "making a bequest" is the same as saying "leaving an inheritance.") Some of us worry too much about leaving money behind when we die. By all means, make sure your spouse's needs are met. And if you are a Cleaver (a Type 2 retiree), then you might also want to set aside some amount for anyone else who looks to you for financial support. After those needs are taken care of, though, ask yourself why you would need to leave money to anyone else. I don't buy the argument, "Isn't that what you're supposed to do?"

Motives Behind a Bequest

The economic literature outlines three basic types of bequests: altruistic, strategic and accidental. The altruistic bequest is the type that usually comes to mind. It involves earmarking a certain amount of money to be left to a loved one—usually one's children—out of love and concern for their welfare. Type 2 retirees (the Cleavers) would certainly have an altruistic bequest in mind. The precise amount being left may be uncertain but the Type 2 retiree knows it should be substantial.

The strategic bequest is more like a payoff. You leave money to a person who provides you with attention or care in your latter years, when your health starts to fail. That person could be a relative or an outsider. A strategic bequest rarely involves an actual written contract, but if your intention is to ensure that the caregiver does a good job, that individual should probably be informed about the bequest.

Finally, there are accidental bequests. The money being inherited in this case is whatever remains unspent at the end of your life. Such a bequest is accidental because either you had no one in mind who should be inheriting from your estate, or you do have someone in mind to receive whatever assets remain but no set amount that you wish to leave them. This is usually the only type of bequest made by Type 4 retirees (the YOLOs). It is also a common type of bequest by Type 1 retirees (the mainstream).

To Make a Bequest or Not

You shouldn't feel guilty if you have not planned an altruistic bequest. Not everyone wants to enrich their adult children, not even the wealthy. U.S. Trust conducted a survey in 2012 of 642 "high net worth" adults. All had at least $3 million in investable assets. The survey results were compiled separately for different age groups, but we will focus solely on the baby boomers. Only 55 percent of them felt it was important to leave money to their children.

Among the 45 percent of baby boomers who did not plan to make a bequest, some of the reasons given were as follows:

- Each generation should earn its own wealth (57 percent gave this reason).

- "I worked hard for my wealth and will want to enjoy it myself" (27 percent gave this reason).

- "I would rather give the money to charity (26 percent gave this reason).

There was a fourth reason, which I will get to shortly. If making a bequest is not a high priority for you, then your decumulation strategy just got that much easier. Your main concern is whether your wealth will produce an income stream that satisfies your regular spending needs, not how much money is left over at the end. In fact, leaving a lot behind could be a sign of a failed strategy, not of success.

Age-Related Bequests

As mentioned above, the survey respondents expressed one other reason for not leaving an inheritance. A great many of them said it was
more "important to invest in their children's success while they were
growing up."

There are different ways to interpret this phrase. One interpretation is that the parents' responsibility does not extend beyond
ensuring that their kids have a good upbringing and get a solid education. Once they graduate from high school, or perhaps university, they
are expected to stand on their own two feet. Under this interpretation,
there would be no bequest at all, except an accidental one.

A less harsh interpretation is that the phrase "growing up" includes the period when the children are young adults; the first few
years on their own when they could most use a helping hand. The
financial burden is often greatest in early adulthood because of stu-
dent loans, the raising of young children and/or paying a sizeable
mortgage.

Most people I know continue to support their grown-up children
in some fashion for at least a few years after they've left home. That
support can take many forms, such as paying their kids' cell phone
bills, subsidizing their rent, bringing them along on vacations or
helping them make a down payment on a first house.

The point for people who subscribe to this strategy is to focus
any financial help in the period when the children really need it.
Whatever money you can give to your children when they are 25 or 30
is going to make a much bigger difference in their lives than it would
if you waited until they are 55 or 60, which is how old they might be
when you die.

Of course, you might not be able to give them any money at all
right now because you need it for your own retirement security. The
one thing you can do in that case is shape your bequest in a way that
maximizes its usefulness. Ideally, the amount of the bequest would
be highest if you die at a youngish age, like 70, when the children are

young adults, and the amount would be much less, or nothing, if you die much later on, when your children are in their 50s or 60s.

Setting aside enough money so you can leave a big death benefit comes at the cost of less retirement income for you. Making the right trade-off is part of a sound decumulation strategy.

Bequests and Home Equity

There is another reason not to worry too much about bequests when considering what investments to make with your financial assets. That reason involves your home.

Few Canadians think of using their home as a financial asset while they are still alive, except to the extent they are prepared to downsize. Downsizing as you get close to retirement can free up a little of the equity in your home and is a commonly used strategy. That aside, the equity in the home tends to stay locked in.

This all changes upon death or, more specifically, upon the death of the last surviving spouse. At that point, the home equity is essentially pure cash. Even for retirees who are keen on making a bequest, it can come from the equity in the home. This means you don't have to hold back on spending your financial assets during your retirement years.

What Carl and Hanna Can Do for Their Children

Let's apply the thinking on bequests to Carl and Hanna. I indirectly introduced their children, Samantha and Arnold, in Chapter 3. "Sam" and "Arnie" had become self-supporting by the time Carl and Hanna were 59 and 56 respectively. Six years later, Carl and Hanna are retiring while Sam and Arnie have young families of their own. They have reasonably good jobs by then but are nevertheless struggling to make ends meet. This is not an uncommon situation for young adults.

Carl and Hanna were good parents and now they have become doting grandparents. If they could help Sam and Arnie out financially, they would, but they still don't know if the $550,000 they saved for their own retirement is going to be enough. There is no point in bankrolling your kids if you are going to end up being a financial burden to them somewhere down the road.

The best they can do for now is to mention Sam and Arnie in their will. If Carl and Hanna both die young, then Sam and Arnie would stand to receive a sizeable inheritance that could help make their lives a lot easier. If Carl and Hanna died in their late 80s or 90s, the bequest from the remaining financial assets might be much smaller but the need for an inheritance should also be smaller. Besides, there is still the equity in the home that could be passed on to Sam and Arnie, unless it is given directly to the grandchildren.

The bottom line is that Carl and Hanna can use their $550,000 to create retirement income for themselves without having to worry too much about bequests. The fewer the constraints imposed on how they invest their financial assets, the easier it will be to devise a smart decumulation strategy.

Takeaways

1. You pay a price for making a large bequest. It can restrict your choice of investment vehicles at retirement and reduce your retirement income.

2. You should be drawing down your financial assets as you get older, which means the bequest you can make will gradually become smaller. This works out well because your children's need for the money should also diminish as they progress into later adulthood.

3. Be clear as to how much money really needs to be passed down to your children. If you or your spouse lives a long time, a bequest may be more useful in the hands of your grandchildren.

4. Don't forget about the equity in the home. It may be locked-in while you are alive, but it can be turned into cash after you and your spouse die. This may be all the inheritance your children will ever need.

7

INVESTMENT RISK

Earthquakes are a common occurrence in California. The Golden State rests on two tectonic plates and the boundary between them forms a fault line, which includes the famous San Andreas Fault. One of the plates is creeping northwest while the other is slowly sliding southeast. The plates create friction as they rub against each other, and sometimes the friction builds up to the point that the two sides become locked and stop moving. The tension this causes eventually becomes great enough to overcome the force of friction. The two plates then snap back into place in a violent motion that we experience as an earthquake.

Earthquakes are inevitable and can cause damage. While the extent of it is usually fairly minor, a more destructive event will occur from time to time, like the 6.7 magnitude Northridge earthquake that struck in the San Fernando Valley near Los Angeles in 1994. As bad as that was, locals know that earthquakes can be even more severe. They fear the coming of the "big one"—a truly massive earthquake like the one that practically demolished San Francisco in 1906.

Investing in stocks is a lot like living on a fault line. You expose yourself to risk every day but you keep on living your life just the same. If a considerable time has elapsed since the last disaster, you might start to worry less. But if the "big one" hits, it could still be catastrophic.

It has been a long while since the last devastating "earthquake" in the stock market. The market collapse that accompanied the 2008–09 financial crisis was quite serious, of course, and many people who were close enough to its epicentre never truly recovered from it. Most investors, though, survived and eventually found prosperity again. The one-day crash of October 19, 1987 was mind-boggling at the time as the Dow Jones index fell 22 percent; but when the dust cleared, the damage was very limited. In each case, investors who kept their heads and stayed fully invested eventually came out on top.

In the past century, there has been just one stock market crash that paralleled the 1906 San Francisco earthquake in terms of the damage it caused. It was the great market crash that started in October 1929. By the time the stock market hit bottom in July 1932, the Dow Jones index had fallen 89 percent. The 1929 peak would not be surpassed until 1954 and by then retirees from the late 1920s were no longer around. This was truly the last "big one."

Is the fear of another market meltdown like the 1929 crash reason enough to steer clear of stocks in retirement? My answer would be an emphatic no.

For one thing, it is unlikely to happen. A disastrous earthquake in California in the foreseeable future is more likely than a comparable stock market crash. According to a US Geological Survey report, there is a 7-percent chance of an earthquake of 8.0 or greater hitting somewhere in California in the next 30 years. Based on Monte Carlo simulations, the probability of a market crash of similar proportions occurring in that time span is just 1 percent or so.

Second, even if it does happen, you will probably come out of it in one piece. Consider the 1929 market crash again. If you had been saving for retirement back then, you wouldn't have invested your entire portfolio in stocks. You might have put 60 percent in Canadian and US stocks and the rest in bonds. With that type of asset mix, a

$10,000 portfolio as of January 1, 1929, would have fallen to $6,000 in real terms (ignoring inflation) by 1933. This sounds bad, but it's a far cry from the 89-percent drop mentioned above.

The $6,000 account balance would have been the low point, as the portfolio would start to grow again after 1933. It would have grown to $14,000 (again, in real terms) by 1937 and to $23,000 by 1949. It is almost as if the crash had never happened!

The clincher is that even the drop in the portfolio to $6,000 is not as bad as it sounds. While it is quite low compared to $10,000, remember that you didn't put $10,000 into the market in the first place. If you had been investing all along, then as of January 1927, your portfolio would have been worth about $6,000 and at that time you would have been reasonably happy with that balance.

To sum up, you would have survived the worst stock market crash in history no worse off than you would have been two or three years before the crash started, assuming you had been investing in a balanced portfolio of stocks and bonds all along.

Alternatives to Stocks

If you don't want to invest in stocks, what would you do instead? Would you turn to real estate? Some people buy multiple condo units and rent them out, for example. This can be profitable when the local housing market is doing well, but disparities from one region to another can be wide, and even robust housing markets don't rise in a straight line forever. Condo investors can lose everything if they hold mortgages on their rental properties and the real estate market cools, especially if interest rates rise at the same time; this happened to many people when the Toronto housing bubble burst in 1989.

Outside of Toronto and Vancouver, the real estate market in Canada is actually fairly sedate. It might still produce good returns in the future, but you face three problems. The first is liquidity. It can take many months to sell a condo, and you cannot afford to be illiquid if you need the money to make ends meet. A second problem is finding a suitable investment if you have only a smallish amount to invest. In the real estate market, even a few hundred thousand dollars is considered small potatoes. Third, transaction costs and property taxes can be considerable. All in all, real estate investing is not for amateurs.

Instead of owning real estate, some people lend out money in private transactions in the form of a second mortgage. They do this to get the extra yield compared to bank deposits, but this practice can be quite dangerous. I know of people who have tried it and lost their capital when the borrower couldn't make the payments.

At the other end of the risk spectrum, you could stay completely liquid and invest only in **T-bills**. This strategy is safe if all you want to do is preserve your capital. Over the long term, though, you are almost certain to do worse with T-bills than with any other asset class. In the decades since 1933, for instance, T-bills have barely beaten inflation. You would have been *much* better off investing in stocks and bonds after 1923 instead of T-bills; this is in spite of the market crash.

Going forward, the prospects for T-bills are even dimmer, as it appears that low interest rates will be with us for a long time. The most likely **nominal** return with T-bills is less than 2 percent a year, and even that is not a sure thing. Current yields are less than 1 percent!

The term **T-bills** is short for Treasury bills. These are short-term investments issued by national governments, including the Government of Canada, to regulate the money supply and to raise funds on the open market. They are offered with terms of 91, 182 and 364 days.

A **nominal** return ignores the effects of inflation. Most people who are not actuaries or investment experts think in nominal terms. The real return is the nominal return less inflation. For instance, a nominal return of 5 percent when inflation is 2 percent means the real return is 3 percent.

What about long-term Government of Canada bonds? Unfortunately, that ship has sailed. They were great investments when interest rates were high and trending downwards, which was the case from the early 1980s until very recently; however, interest rates have since bottomed out. For the next few years, rates might stay low or they might slowly start to trend upwards. The one thing they cannot do is go much lower. It may be counterintuitive, but rising interest rates create losses, not gains, if you are holding long-term bonds.

Consider the early 1950s, which is the last time interest rates and inflation were both low for a number of years. If you invested in long-term government bonds starting in January 1953 and continued until the end of 1981, your average annual return in nominal terms would have been 3.1 percent, but you would have lost about 50 percent of your initial investment in real terms. (If you had invested in Canadian stocks during the same 29-year period, you would have quintupled your money in real terms!)

Finally, you might consider real return bonds. These are also long-term bonds issued by the Government of Canada. What makes them different from regular bonds is that they promise a real return, regardless of whether the inflation rate goes up or down. The problem is that the real yield on these bonds has been less than 1 percent in recent years—a far cry from the 1990s when real interest rates exceeded 4 percent. The one positive aspect of real return bonds is that they can be bought and sold easily. Just be aware that you would suffer a capital loss if real interest rates were to rise after you bought the bonds. You might want to find some room in your RRIF for real return bonds; but given where we are today, I believe the allocation should be fairly small.

The inescapable conclusion is that you have to invest in stocks if you want a decent return over the long run. There is no guarantee you will get it, but your odds are better than with any other asset class. Even if the "big one" hits capital markets during your lifetime, you will probably recoup most, if not all, of your losses if you hang in there long enough.

What to Expect from a Portfolio of Stocks and Bonds

If you do end up investing a significant percentage of your savings in stocks, you might like to know the possible range of results. To this end, I had the Morneau Shepell actuarial team run a **Monte Carlo simulation.**

I described **Monte Carlo simulations** at length in my last book and so will spare readers another description here except to say that a Monte Carlo simulation is a very sophisticated computer program that is used to figure out how something complex might behave. For input, it has to rely on historical patterns and correlations between asset classes.

Before we look at the results of the simulation, let me start with the following caveats:

- No one knows the future. Any investment manager who tells you he or she knows where the stock market is headed is not being honest. Even the Monte Carlo simulations used in this book are only as good as what is input into the computer model.

- Based on stock market performance over the past century, we know equities will have their good years and their bad years; we just don't know when. We know a little more about how bonds behave, but not much more.

- Certain "black swan" events have occurred in the past, like world wars and major oil shocks.* No doubt more such events will occur in the future, and they may be different than anything we have seen so far and could have a major impact on stocks or bonds. Unfortunately, there is no good way to build black swan events into our planning.

---

* It was Nassim Nicholas Taleb who coined the term black swan. It means a disruptive event that cannot have been foreseen.

- In the projections, I have assumed that inflation will remain steady at 2.2 percent a year, although most of the time it will be higher or lower than that.

"When will we see the next one?"

Keeping these disclaimers in mind, Figure 7.1 shows the range of investment returns for a portfolio that is invested 50 percent in stocks and 50 percent in bonds.*

Figure 7.1: Range of Results for a 50-50 Asset Mix

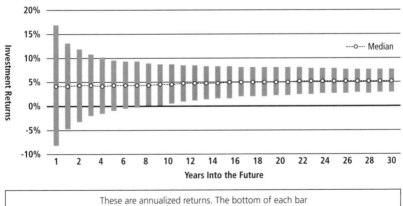

These are annualized returns. The bottom of each bar is the 5th percentile, and the top is the 95th.

---

* The 50% in stocks is assumed to be invested in the S&P/TSX Capped Composite Index and the MSCI World Index.

The bottom of the range is the worst-case scenario that claimed Carl and Hanna as its victims in Chapter 1. The top of the range is a best-case scenario. Take a moment to study Figure 7.1, as it captures most of the investment outcomes that you might possibly face with a 50-50 asset mix. After 10 years, for example, the best-case scenario is an **annualized** (nominal) **return** of 8.8 percent. In the worst case, the annualized return would be a negative 1.4 percent while the **median** return would be 4.5 percent. All of these figures are before investment fees.

Annualized return, over a given period, is the average annual return that if compounded produces the same result as the actual returns over that period. For instance, if actual returns are 2 percent in Year 1 and 10 percent in Year 2, the annualized return for the 2-year period is 5.92 percent. The **median** return is the halfway point of all returns produced by the Monte Carlo simulation.

Note, by the way, that the "worst case" actually isn't quite the very worst. There is still a chance in 20 that investment returns can be lower. Similarly, there is a chance in 20 that the results can be better than the "best case" result. It is customary with Monte Carlo simulations to ignore the "tails" of the distribution because they stretch out so far.

Here are a few observations based on the chart:

- Even under the worst-case scenario, you should expect positive returns if you invest for long enough; in this case, for nine years or longer.

- The gap between the best-case and the worst-case scenarios narrows over time, but the two scenarios never converge.

- The median return is surprisingly low. In the long run, it is expected to be just a shade over 5 percent, and this is before deducting investment fees.

The last point bears emphasizing. A long-term median return in the 5-percent range is a far cry from the 8.6-percent return that the median pension fund manager actually earned between 1960 and 2015. There are several reasons why future stock market returns will be lower than we are used to seeing. One is that inflation will probably be closer to 2 percent rather than the average of nearly 4 percent that has prevailed since 1960. Another is that pension fund managers invest about 60 percent in equities rather than 50 percent. A third reason is that the bond portion of portfolios will probably not do as well in the future because interest rates are so low.

The Investment Problems of Main Street

The foregoing assumes readers have some experience with investing in stocks and bonds. For some readers, though, this analysis does not begin to describe the investment problems that they actually face. The survey that was reported in Chapter 5 gave us a hint of what these investment-related problems look like and, for the most part, they have little to do with regular investments in stocks or bonds.

One of the shocks feared by many of the people surveyed was a drop in the value of their home of 25 percent or more. This could distress homeowners of any age, but the only way it should affect your retirement security is if you took out a mortgage or a home equity loan. With very few exceptions, which I will describe in Chapter 16, borrowing against your home in retirement is a bad idea. If you don't do that, this type of shock should not concern you too much.

Another shock that was described in the survey was the loss of one's home through foreclosure. If you pay off your mortgage by retirement age and subsequently resist the urge to take out a home equity line of credit, then this shouldn't happen. There are few good reasons for going back into debt after retirement.

Two shocks that relate more directly to financial investments include running out of assets and incurring a loss in the total value of your investable assets of 10 percent or more. In either of these situations, the retiree probably invested in a specific stock rather than in a bigger pool of stocks or bonds. I strongly suggest that retirees invest only in a pool, such as a mutual fund or an index that one can buy in the form of an ETF (described in Chapter 10). Don't become a stock-picker or day trader and don't buy some highflier on the tip of a friend. The odds are very much against you. Even a broker's recommendations are unlikely to be better than random.

I used to research the market on my own and trade in individual stocks. It was hubris to think I was smarter than the crowd and could make profits on a consistent basis by taking a contrarian stance. Over time, I did pick a few winners, but I also picked way too many losers. I didn't beat the market anywhere nearly often enough to call the experience a success. Today, I invest only in the pooled funds of an institutional manager. I picked an investment manager who is part of a major bank, because they are not apt to "go rogue" on me. I don't want anyone to take unnecessary risks with my investments.

More to Come

This isn't the last word on investment risk. Chapter 13 will explore the question of what asset mix is appropriate once you are in decumulation mode.

Takeaways

1. It is hard to avoid investing in stocks if you want a decent return on your savings.

2. If you have a diversified portfolio of stocks and bonds, you will probably be able to survive even a market disaster as severe as the crash of 1929.

3. Stay away from investing in second mortgages.

4. Real estate investment can be lucrative for long-term investors, but it is not for amateurs.

5. You might invest some of your savings in T-bills or other short-term investments but only a smallish portion. The same goes with real return bonds.

6. Long-term Government of Canada bonds are unlikely to do well for many years to come, but they still tend to form part of most investment portfolios.

7. The median return on a portfolio of stocks and bonds is likely to be just 5 to 5.5 percent a year in the longer term, and this is before fees.

8. Since we seem to be mired in an environment of low interest rates and low investment returns for the long term, you cannot afford to pay a lot in investment fees.

9. Invest only in pooled funds or ETFs that represent the entire market. Don't try to pick your own stocks, even with the help of a broker.

8

WHAT NOT TO DO

In Chapter 1, we saw what happened when Carl and Hanna drew down their savings based on the widely accepted 4-percent rule. They ran out of money by age 83. After that, government pensions were their only source of income. Living solely on government pensions is not so bad if you never knew any better, but you wouldn't want to try it if you were used to having investable assets.

Certainly, Carl and Hanna weren't helped by the capital markets that gave them such lousy investment results, but this wasn't their only problem. Investment losses will happen from time to time and a good decumulation strategy will take the bad times in stride. The bigger problem was using the 4-percent rule to set their spending rate.

It is important to understand that the 4-percent rule failed Carl and Hanna in more ways than one. Running out of money stands out as the main reason, of course, but there was another significant shortcoming. The amount of income under the 4-percent rule did not reflect the couple's retirement income target. It generated too much money in some years and not enough in others.

We calculated the income target for Carl and Hanna in chapters 3 and 4. Actually, they had a *range* of targets, with the top end of the range being the amount of income they would really like, and the bottom end allowing for at least a tolerable existence. I called this range the acceptable zone. A good decumulation strategy would produce income somewhere within this zone even if the investments fail to perform well.

It is a little unfair to single out the 4-percent rule for criticism. After all, you can get into trouble with a number of other decumulation strategies that are also quite popular. We'll run through them one by one so that you can recognize those strategies and the pitfalls they present. You never know when you might run into one of them. In the illustrations below, I will assume that Carl and Hanna both live until their 90s. This isn't necessarily realistic, but it removes the "noise" of considering what happens when a spouse dies at a younger age. That is an important question, of course, but not for the purposes of rejecting certain decumulation strategies.

Rejected Strategy 1—Withdraw a Flat Percentage

Some retirees find that withdrawing an ever-increasing percentage of their assets each year is a frightening prospect. They would prefer to draw an annual income equal to a flat percentage of their assets instead. For instance, it might be 5 percent or 6 percent of the RRIF account balance as of the end of the previous year. A flat percentage is easy to understand and you can never run out of money.

The obvious problem with a flat percentage is that it runs afoul of the RRIF rules regarding minimum withdrawals (described later in this chapter). If you choose 5 percent, for example, you will be offside by age 71 when the minimum RRIF withdrawal percentage is 5.28 percent (and rising). Choose 6 percent and you are offside by age 77.

You can work around this problem by taking a portion of the monies that you are required to withdraw from the RRIF each year and redepositing it into a TFSA or a bank account. Note that the unspent amount cannot go back into the RRIF, and if you have no employment income it can't go into an RRSP either. Since the money was withdrawn from a RRIF (or LIF), you have to pay income tax on it, even if you did not spend all of it that year. As a result, there may not be as much to redeposit as you would like.

The real problem with a flat percentage withdrawal is that the income it produces does not reflect your actual needs. This can be seen in Figure 8.1, where we assume that 6 percent of total assets is withdrawn from savings each year. Even though I am assuming median investment returns, Carl and Hanna have income above their target only for the first four or five years. Their income is below their target from age 70 right up until age 95, even though they still have more than $200,000 left in their account at that point. While the simplicity of flat percentage withdrawals is seductive, I don't think you should consider it.

Figure 8.1: Drawing Down a Flat 6% Each Year

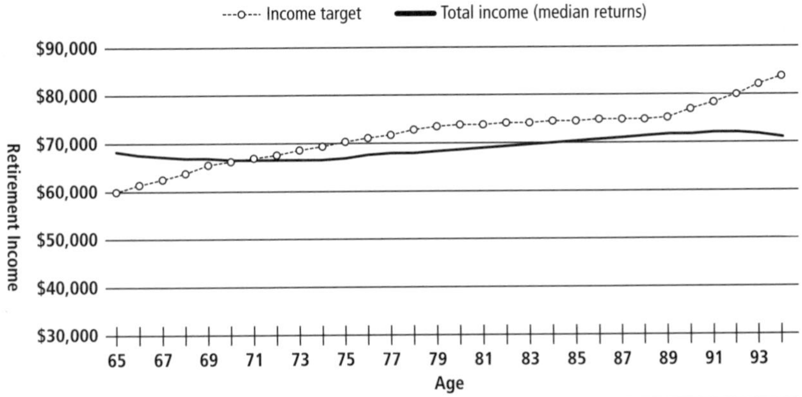

Drawing the same percentage each year leaves a lot of money on the table and does not track the income target very well.

Rejected Strategy 2—Withdraw Only the Interest

According to one professional survey, only two people in ten intend to spend down their assets in retirement.[1] The rest of them try to live off the interest or even hope to continue growing their assets after retirement. Apparently, most people really hate to touch their principal.

A decumulation strategy in which one spends only the investment income might work out for people who have minimal assets and are ready to limit spending to what their CPP and OAS pensions can buy. They cannot afford to part with much of their capital because they might need it for a rainy day situation.

Spending only the investment income might also make some sense for the lucky retirees whose investment income is in the six figures. The investment income alone might give them a comfortable lifestyle and enable them to leave a large bequest.

For middle-income people like Carl and Hanna, however, an interest-only strategy makes little sense. Figure 8.2 shows why. It uses actual investment returns and inflation from 1952 to 1986 to show just how volatile investment income can be. In some years they will have much more income than their target and in other years much less. (I used this period because inflation and interest rates were low at the start of it, so it bears some resemblance to the current economic

Figure 8.2: Withdrawing Only the Investment Return

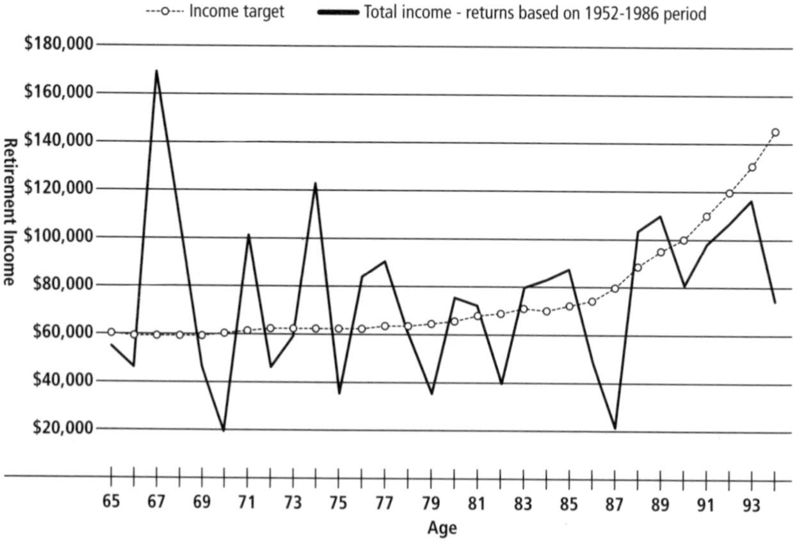

The chart assumes that the annual withdrawal includes interest plus gains and losses. The returns and inflation rates were taken from the 1952–86 period to simulate real-life conditions. Income includes CPP and OAS based on modern levels.

environment.) In years where there is a net investment loss, I got around the RRIF minimum withdrawal rules by assuming the withdrawn amounts would be redeposited rather than being spent.

I suppose Carl and Hanna could have made this decumulation strategy work better by banking the excess return in good years (i.e., ages 67, 71 and 74), but that would have increased the unspent amount at the end of their lives. I can somewhat understand the popularity of this strategy. It is a crude form of risk management for people who don't know what they don't know, but there are better decumulation strategies out there.

Default Option—Make the Minimum Permitted Withdrawal

Under the simplest decumulation strategy, you do what the government says you must do with tax-sheltered savings. Income tax regulations specify the minimum percentage of your total assets that you *must* withdraw each year if your money is in a RRIF or a LIF. The minimum at age 65 is 4 percent. It rises in steps to 5 percent at age 70, 6.82 percent at 80 and 11.92 percent at 90. The minimum finally plateaus at age 95 at 20 percent. You do have the option to withdraw more in any year, but you cannot withdraw less. Details on the minimum and maximum limits are given in Appendix B.

Of course, the fact you withdraw a given percentage of your assets does not mean you have to spend it all. You could always choose to spend less and redeposit the rest. This possibility was mentioned earlier as was the problem that there would be a little "shrinkage" due to income tax being payable on the withdrawn amounts.

While it is included in this chapter among the flawed decumulation strategies, withdrawing the minimum amount each year actually produces a pretty good pattern of income. In the case of median investment returns, the income that Carl and Hanna receive is close to their income target. This is shown in Figure 8.3.

Figure 8.3: Making the Minimum RRIF Withdrawal

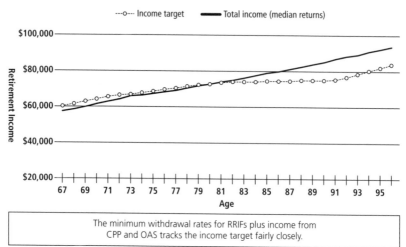

The minimum withdrawal rates for RRIFs plus income from
CPP and OAS tracks the income target fairly closely.

This may seem like quibbling, but this RRIF minimum withdrawal strategy can still be improved. (Maybe I would like it better if I had thought of it rather than the federal government.) For one thing, it encourages retirees to underspend in their early retirement years, which is a time when they could really enjoy the money. Once again, better strategies exist.

Withdrawing Income Equal to the Target

All of the above strategies involve withdrawing an amount that is somehow based on the available assets. That basic principle sounds perfectly reasonable, but it would be so much better to be able to withdraw an amount equal to the income target. After all, you know roughly how much you need to maintain a certain lifestyle and you don't want to give up the things you love if you don't have to.

The problem with drawing income based on needs rather than assets is obvious. How will you know if your money will last a lifetime? The answer is, you don't; at least not yet. We will see in Chapter 9 that if Carl and Hanna try drawing income equal to their income target, their savings will run out by age 79. That outcome is even worse than what the 4-percent rule produced in Chapter 1!

Obviously, you cannot draw the income you want without taking into account the assets you have. At this point, you might be tempted to stick with the RRIF minimum withdrawal strategy that was mentioned above, but let's not settle for a mediocre outcome. You can do better.

To do so, you need to find a way to incorporate both your income target and your available assets into the decumulation strategy, sort of like watching the speedometer and keeping an eye on the fuel gauge at the same time. This is what Part II is all about.

Takeaways

1. Investment losses will happen every so often; a good decumulation strategy should be able to absorb them.

2. Withdrawing the minimum amount permitted under the RRIF rules is not a bad approach to decumulation, but the chapters to come will show you can do better.

3. Withdrawing the same percentage of assets each year does not work well. In general, you should expect to withdraw an increasing percentage with age.

4. You may be tempted to spend only the investment income and leave the principal intact, but this strategy makes sense only at the extremes of wealth. It is not recommended for those in the middle-income range.

5. You need to find a way to incorporate both your income target and your available assets into your decumulation strategy—not just one or the other.

PART II

THE STRATEGY

9

AN OVERVIEW OF THE STRATEGY

In a 2017 interview for Bloomberg News, Warren Buffett said, "Money has no utility to me; time has utility." Money, of course, has a lot of utility to most other people, but we can still learn something from Buffett's words. Even for people of modest means, the utility of money decreases the more you have. This rule has implications for one's choice of investments when carrying out a decumulation strategy.

In Chapter 3, I showed how Carl and Hanna set their retirement income target at $60,000 a year. If they suffered investment losses in retirement that brought their income down to $45,000, this could make a big dent in their lifestyle. They would probably muddle through, but it wouldn't be pleasant.

If they came into a windfall that increased their income from $60,000 to $75,000, they could suddenly spend money in ways that were not previously possible. Even so, the sad truth is that the pleasure that comes from increasing income by $15,000 does not match the pain from seeing it drop by a like amount. In his work, Daniel Kahneman has pointed out this fundamental asymmetry in our lives: we suffer from a loss much more than we enjoy a windfall of the same magnitude.* This is why I'm giving up on Las Vegas.

---

* Kahneman is a psychologist known for his work in behavioral economics and is the author of the book *Thinking, Fast and Slow.*

The conclusion is that you don't want to take big risks within your decumulation strategy. By definition, a risk might not pay off, so you have to ask yourself if you can handle the resulting loss, either financially or emotionally. We need to keep this in mind as I unfold the full decumulation strategy in this Part II.

The ultimate goal is to "win," but what does winning look like in the decumulation arena? The foregoing chapters should have given us a glimpse. For Carl and Hanna, winning involves fulfilling the following goals:

- Having enough money to continue the same level of regular spending as they enjoyed before they retired.

- Accepting the optimal amount of financial uncertainty. They cannot always expect to hit their income target if they invest in stocks; however, as I pointed out, they really have no choice if they want to realize decent returns. As a result of investing in the stock market, they might fall a little short of their target every so often, which is fine as long as their income remains within their acceptable zone.

- Not outliving their savings. Decumulation is a balancing act between drawing sufficient income and ensuring one's account balance does not diminish too quickly.

- Being able to cope with rainy day situations. For that purpose, they plan to hold back a smallish percentage of their retirement income each year and keep it in a reserve fund until that rainy day arrives.

- Making room for bequests. Since Carl and Hanna have limited financial resources, a bequest is the only way they can help their adult children financially. The size of that bequest will shrink over time as they draw down their assets, but the needs of Sam and Arnie, who are now approaching their own retirement, should also shrink.

The game plan is to draw income equal to Carl and Hanna's chosen income target, but there needs to be some flexibility to adjust their spending depending on how the future unfolds. Figure 9.1 shows the result before we start putting the decumulation strategy in place. This is our baseline.

Figure 9.1: Drawing Income Equal to the Income Target

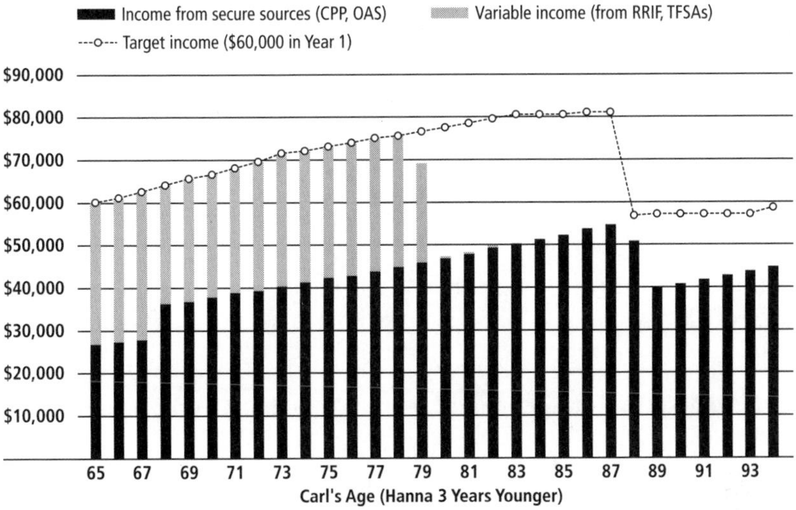

This is the "Before" picture. With no strategy, $550,000 worth of RRIF and TFSA assets runs out when Carl is 79. The income target falls by 30% at age 88 when Carl dies.

It would appear that we have taken a big step backwards. Unlike the RRIF minimum withdrawal approach, Carl and Hanna used up their entire savings very quickly by drawing income equal to the income target. The only income they have left after age 80 comes from their CPP and OAS pensions. This is an even worse result than they got with the 4-percent rule!

Obviously we need to enhance this strategy. Basically, Carl and Hanna want to ensure their money lasts for life while remaining in the acceptable zone even if their investments do badly. How they accomplish this will be the focus of the next seven chapters.

Overview of the Enhancements

The reader will eventually become acquainted with five basic enhancements to the very rudimentary decumulation strategy that is illustrated in Figure 9.1. While some of the enhancements are no-brainers, some of them you may not like and at least one (Enhancement 5) may prove to be unnecessary if all goes well. Here is a brief overview of the enhancements:

Enhancement 1: Carl and Hanna exchange their actively managed mutual funds for much less expensive funds that are passively managed. By doing so, they significantly reduce the annual investment fees they are paying and they're not giving anything up to do so. The result is a significant increase in the amount of income they can derive from their savings.

The next three enhancements all have something in common: while they reduce upside potential when the capital markets do exceptionally well, they also reduce downside risk (which is good). This trade-off might not sound momentous, but Carl and Hanna are gaining something very precious: income protection when they really need it. Anyone who lived through the 2008–09 financial crisis with market-based assets will know only too well that risk is more than a four-letter word.

Enhancement 2: They start their CPP pensions at age 70 instead of 65. It would be a gross understatement to say this tactic has not caught on with Canadians, but it is more effective than people realize. Deferral increases the total retirement income that Carl and Hanna can expect and reduces investment risk and **longevity risk** at the same time. It is like an insurance policy that costs you nothing. This cost-free insurance is possible because the CPP administration is generous with the increases in pensions that are granted when the starting age is postponed.

Longevity risk is the risk of running out of money as a result of living longer than expected.

Enhancement 3: Carl and Hanna use some of their RRIF assets to purchase an annuity. I know that annuities are almost as unpopular as deferring CPP, but it's important to give this insurance product another look. I will show that an annuity purchase using just 30 percent of their savings will help Carl and Hanna to close in on the goals listed at the start of this chapter.

Enhancement 4: This enhancement is different from all the previous ones. It asks Carl and Hanna to make some adjustments to their spending habits rather than to their investments. They will adjust their spending up or down as their financial health changes. This will help to keep their income within their acceptable income zone when the first three enhancements aren't quite enough to get the job done.

Enhancement 5: The fifth and final enhancement is the most controversial one of the lot, but I believe it has to be on the table under certain circumstances. If Carl and Hanna cannot generate enough income, they would need to consider taking out a reverse mortgage (the so-called "nuclear option")

Going through the Checklist

You are probably eager to dive into the enhancements, but first let's ensure you are starting from the right place. If you have been doing the right things to prepare for retirement, the following list should describe your situation at the point of retirement:

☐ **You have paid off the mortgage on your house.** If you still have a sizeable mortgage, you might not be retirement-ready. Yes, the interest rate on mortgages is low these days, but the risk-free interest you are earning on bank accounts or fixed income investments in your portfolio is lower still.

☐ **You are paying off your credit cards each month.** The worst thing you can do is to carry over unpaid balances into the following month because the credit card companies are charging you interest at close to 20 percent a year.

☐ **You are not using a home equity line of credit to supplement your regular spending needs.** It is always a good idea to live within your means, but in retirement it is absolutely essential. Using a home equity line of credit to augment your spending suggests you are not living within your means, and this is dangerous.

☐ **Your children are self-supporting.** It is quite possible you are still helping them out financially, and as long as you have included this obligation in your regular spending as it was defined in Chapter 2, then all is well.

☐ **Most of your savings are held in tax-assisted vehicles like an RRSP (which becomes a RRIF after retirement) or a defined contribution pension plan (which might become a LIF after retirement).** This is not to say there is anything wrong with having assets outside of a RRIF or a LIF. The fact that your non-registered assets, which were accumulated with after-tax dollars, will not be taxed when you use them to produce income is a good thing. See Chapter 19 for more on this subject.

☐ **Your investments are not locked-in.** Some mutual funds come with deferred sales charges (DSCs). The purpose of these is to pay the mutual fund salesperson upfront, but the result is very negative for the investor since one's freedom to act is severely restricted.

Takeaways

1. Money has diminishing utility the higher your income level. It is more important to avoid falling short than it is to generate excess income.

2. A good starting point for a decumulation strategy is the RRIF minimum withdrawal schedule. But you need to enhance it to better reflect your income needs.

10

ENHANCEMENT 1
REDUCING FEES

We are ready for Enhancement 1 to your decumulation strategy. It involves picking investment funds with low investment management fees. You will recall that Carl and Hanna invested their RRIF assets in mutual funds with a total annual fee of 1.8 percent. (This fee is also known as the **management expense ratio** or **MER**.) I will try to get it down to just a fraction of that number—about 0.5 percent (which is 50 basis points).

Management expense ratio (MER) is the total percentage of assets the investment company charges you in a given year to cover investment, administrative and sales-related other charges. For example, an MER of 1.8 percent on assets of $500,000 results in annual expenses of $9,000. In the case of mutual funds, these fees are quietly deducted from the assets.

You might well ask whether Carl and Hanna are giving something up by choosing investment funds that cost them barely a quarter of what they are paying now. I don't think they are, but we will get into that later on.

By the way, their investment fees could have been much higher. The MER on some mutual funds can top 3 percent when you tack on the fee that a financial advisor typically charges. When your total expected return before fees is just 5 percent or so, this is a lot to give up. Remember that the first 2 percent simply covers inflation. A fee of 3 percent on a portfolio that is earning just 5 percent means that your investment fund manager and your financial advisor are scooping up *all* of the real growth in your portfolio.

ETFs

To bring their fees down to just 50 basis points, Carl and Hanna will need to abandon typical retail mutual fund products and go with **exchange-traded funds (ETFs)**. The ETFs I have in mind are **passively** managed investments. They are increasingly popular because the fees tend to be much lower than is the case with **active management**. In addition, ETFs are easy to buy and sell.

Exchange-traded funds (ETFs) are funds that track a stock or bond index. They are different from a similar-looking mutual fund or pooled fund in that they can be traded on a stock exchange, the same as any common stock.

Passive management in an investment context means an investment that is meant to mimic an index that represents the entire market or some subset of the market. There is no attempt to beat the market with passively managed funds. The alternative is **active management**, whereby the manager does try to beat the market.

You have to be careful, though, when picking your ETFs. To test out the user experience, I went online to the site of one of Canada's Big Five banks to look at their ETF offering. I found it a little confusing to navigate the first time, and I'm in the business! Both the website and the live chat line that the bank offered seemed to be steering me, the user, to pick an ETF that would include the help of a financial advisor. This is certainly the easiest way to do it, and maybe even the smartest way if you are not investment savvy, but you get hit with a hefty advisor charge on top of the MER for the ETF itself. In fact, the fee the advisor would charge on an ongoing basis can easily exceed the charge for the ETFs themselves.

If you try to construct your own ETF portfolio without the help of an advisor, you need to know what you are doing, as there is a mind-boggling array of ETFs on offer. Some of these are very basic, like the S&P/TSX Capped Composite, which tracks the performance of the Toronto Stock Exchange. By the way, this particular fund should probably form the core of your portfolio. It has the added attraction of sporting an annual MER of less than 10 basis points.

Other ETFs are quite exotic, like the US High Dividend Covered Call ETF or the US Put Write ETF. Only experts should consider investing in these. By the way, you will also come across some actively managed ETFs for which the fees are a lot higher than they are for the passively managed ETFs. To my mind, they seem to defeat the purpose of considering an ETF in the first place, so I will leave it to the banks to explain their raison d'être.

Carl and Hanna were brave enough to put together their own ETF portfolio. Using the bank's website, they chose some fairly basic ETFs to create a portfolio that is weighted 50 percent in stocks and 50 percent in bonds. Table 10.1 shows what they came up with.

Table 10.1: Fees for an ETF Portfolio

Asset Class	% of Total Portfolio	MER
Canadian stocks (S&P/TSX Capped Composite ETF)	30%	.06%
US stocks (S&P 500 ETF)	20%	.11%
Canadian bonds (Aggregate Bond Index ETF)	45%	.23%
Cash equivalent (Ultra Short-Term Bond ETF)	5%	.17%
Total portfolio	**100%**	**.152%**

Their portfolio has an annual MER of just 15.2 basis points. This is obviously a lot less than 50 basis points, but later on Carl and Hanna might want to add an ETF that is invested in equities outside of North America for greater diversification. Such a product typically comes with an MER of 60 or 70 basis points, which will bring up the average. In addition, they will be incurring expenses for trading, reporting and custodial fees, and those expenses should also be taken into account. The total should still be under 50 basis points. In any event, it is a far cry from the 180 basis points that they incurred with their original portfolio.

By the way, Carl and Hanna will have to engage in some buying and selling of their ETFs just to keep the asset mix the same as what they initially chose. It is not uncommon to see one asset class (such as Canadian stocks) rise much faster than another (such as Canadian bonds), and if the portfolio is not rebalanced, the asset mix will quietly start to drift away from the 50-50 mix they started with. This is not only dangerous; it is a missed opportunity. The Canadian Institute of Actuaries (CIA) confirms that rebalancing the asset mix on a regular basis is a good idea. Once a quarter would be frequent enough. Over the long run, this practice can add up to 50 basis points of annual return to a portfolio. This is as close as you will ever come to a free lunch in the investment world.

At this point, it is a fair question to ask whether Carl and Hanna should really be trying to create a portfolio on their own. They did it on their own in order to keep fees down, but do they know enough to avoid all the pitfalls? I made the generous assumption that they have more financial acumen than the average person, or at least Hanna does. She has been reading up on investments for the past couple of years in an effort to better understand the risks and opportunities. She has also bounced her ideas off friends who are in the financial industry in some capacity. Nevertheless, this DIY approach sounds potentially dangerous, and it is, but I will defer the subject of whether to go it alone until Chapter 20. For now, let us assume that Carl and Hanna succeed in implementing their low-cost investment portfolio.

Does Active Management Add Value?

Getting back to an earlier question, will a portfolio consisting of ETFs perform as well as an actively managed portfolio? You would think there would be a clear and concise answer to this question, but if so, it is hard to find. Certainly, the professional investment managers will claim to add value, but they are hard-pressed to show it over the long term.

A good place to find hard data on the subject is in the SPIVA Canada Scorecard, which is published every six months. To quote from this publication, "The SPIVA Canada Scorecard reports on the performance of actively managed Canadian mutual funds versus that of their benchmarks."

Looking at the Scorecard for year-end 2016, Table 10.2 shows the percentage of managers in each category who outperformed their respective benchmark over the 12 months ending December 31, 2016.

**Table 10.2: Percent of Managers Outperforming
Their Benchmark**

Canadian equity	17.3%
Canadian dividend and income	19.4%
US equity	28.4%
International equity	23.8%
Global equity	24.1%

If performance is random, you would still expect some managers to beat their benchmark every year, simply out of luck. If active management added value, the percentage of managers who outperform their benchmark should be a lot higher than 25 percent. The fact that just one-fifth to one-quarter of the managers outperformed their benchmark is not a sign of skill.

Lest you think that 2016 was an anomaly, here is a direct quote from SPIVA Canada's year-end 2016 scorecard:

Over the longer term, such as the five-year investment horizon, the results are unequivocal across all domestic equity categories. The data show the losing pattern repeating across all categories, as the majority of active managers underperformed their respective benchmarks. The addition of a 10-year period shows further struggles for active managers, with less than one quarter of funds outperforming.

The inability to beat the markets consistently comes down to the efficiency of the markets, which means their ability to reflect all available information in the current prices of securities.

Burton Malkiel famously claimed that a monkey throwing darts could select stocks as well as investment managers.* A serious investment journal tested this claim and reported the results in a paper that was published in 2013.[1] The authors found that inverting the algorithms behind popular, well-established stock-picking strategies provided equal or better performance. They further concluded that the same is true with any random stock-selection strategy. In other words, you could follow a given approach or do precisely the opposite and it won't make a significant difference in the long run. If that doesn't suggest randomness, I don't know what does!

Even an august body such as the Canadian Institute of Actuaries (the only CIA we'll refer to in this book) has albeit implicitly expressed skepticism about the advantages of active management. In their official guidance to actuaries for the purpose of estimating the long-term return on a portfolio, the CIA essentially puts the onus on the actuary to demonstrate that active management will enhance returns over the long run beyond the fees that are charged. Few actuaries are up to that challenge. Morneau Shepell is a firm with over one hundred actuaries who perform valuations for hundreds of pension plans; not one of those actuaries tries to prove that active management adds value beyond the fees charged.

The chart in Chapter 7 illustrated the range of returns one can expect from a 50-50 asset mix. We need to reduce those returns now to reflect the investment management fee of 50 basis points. The result is shown in Figure 10.1.

The chart shows that the net return investors can expect from a 50-50 portfolio is barely 5 percent per annum (the median return in the chart), and this is if investment management fees are only 50

---

* Malkiel is author of the brilliant book *A Random Walk Down Wall Street*, first published in 1973 by W.W. Norton & Company.

basis points. If fees were still 180 basis points, the median return would be less than 4 percent.

Figure 10.1: Range of Results for a 50-50 Asset Mix

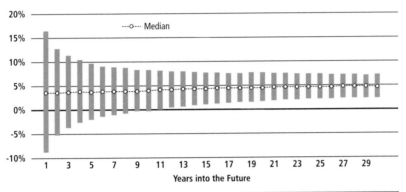

Years into the Future

This shows the range of returns from the 5th to the 95th percentile over different periods. These returns are net of an annual fee of 50 bps.

Unfortunately, returns are expected to be low for a long time to come, whether you manage your money actively or passively. This trend is more the result of an ageing population than it is the lingering effects of the 2008–09 global financial meltdown. An ageing population is dominated by savers rather than borrowers. The result is lower interest rates as well as lower investment returns for a long time to come. Japan is a great example that such a phenomenon can last for decades.

Impact of Lower Fees

Getting back to the issue at hand, we want to see how this 130-basis-point reduction in investment fees translates into more retirement income for Carl and Hanna. The result is shown in Figure 10.2. The grey portion of the bars shows the income from the RRIF and TFSA after investment fees are reduced. We can see that the RRIF and TFSA assets run dry at age 82, and while that's far from perfect, a comparison with Figure 9.1 shows that those assets now last almost two years longer than they did when fees were higher.

Figure 10.2: After Enhancement 1: Reducing Fees

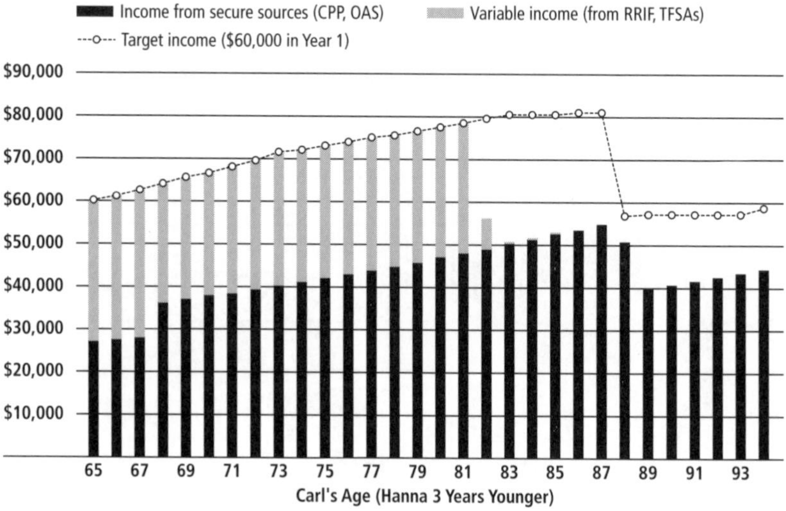

This is identical to Figure 9.1 except that (a) fees have been reduced from 180 bps to 50 bps and (b) spending shocks 2 and 3 were absorbed by a rainy day fund.

Although the picture is a little brighter for Carl and Hanna as a direct result of reducing their investment fees, there is still a shortfall between their actual income and their income target. The next enhancement will make a big difference.

Takeaways

1. Investment fees can have a big impact on how much retirement income one can generate from a given amount of savings.

2. Fees for actively managed mutual funds typically range from 1.5 percent a year to more than 3 percent, depending on the fund family and whether a financial advisor is involved.

3. Tangible evidence of added value from active management is hard to find.

4. Using passively managed ETFs, the total annual investment fee can be brought down to about 50 basis points, if not lower.

11

ENHANCEMENT 2
DEFERRING CPP PENSION

Almost every big bank survey confirms that the biggest concern among retirees (after their health) is outliving their savings. And why wouldn't they be concerned? We have seen that even people who plan responsibly for retirement can lose their entire nest egg long before they die. Enhancement 1 helped Carl and Hanna stretch their retirement dollars a couple more years, but it wasn't enough. They still ended up with only their CPP and OAS pensions after age 82.

What would help is a bigger guaranteed income. The CPP pension is a great example of the ideal benefit. It is fully indexed to inflation and is sure to be paid. The only problem is that it's not nearly enough to meet the needs of a middle-income household. The maximum amount payable at age 65 is just $13,370 a year.*

But what if you could increase your CPP pension by 50 percent? It sounds like a no-brainer—getting a bigger CPP pension that is inflation-protected and paid for life. It will not totally eliminate your income worries, but it would go a long way in that direction. Even if worse comes to worst and your savings run out at some point, the

---

* The maximum payable to someone who reaches age 65 in 2017.

larger CPP payments will ensure that you never slip into outright poverty. This, in a nutshell, is Enhancement 2.

There is only one catch. To get the larger payments you have to forgo receiving CPP pension benefits until you turn 70. Government statistics show that almost no one likes the idea of waiting that long to start their CPP pension; only 1 percent or so of all CPP recipients postpone the start of their CPP payments until age 70. As for that 1 percent, I have to wonder if they started their CPP pension late by design or by accident. Perhaps they simply didn't get around to completing the necessary paperwork sooner!

If so few people intentionally defer their CPP payments until age 70, it is fair to ask if it's really a good idea after all. I will try to convince you it is, but first, let me explain the basic CPP rules. I must warn you, though: you will probably find the next section about as exciting as an explanation of baseball's infield fly rule.

How CPP Pension Is Calculated

From ages 18 to 65, you are required to contribute to the CPP in any year that you earn at least $3,500 with any one employer. You contribute only on employment earnings between $3,500 and a ceiling that approximates the national average wage. In 2017, that ceiling is $55,300. It will continue to rise each year at the same pace as the increases in the average national wage. (We will ignore the recently announced expansion of the Canada Pension Plan because it has little or no effect on people who are retiring in the next 10 years.)

There are 47 potential years of contribution between ages 18 and 65. You have to contribute the maximum amount in only 39 of them to receive a full CPP pension at age 65. In other words, you get to drop out eight years of low or no earnings for purposes of the pension calculation. The dropout period is even longer in special cases, such as for people who stayed at home to raise young children.

In Carl's case, he had no significant employment earnings until age 24; hence no CPP contributions for the first six years of the 47-year period. Later on, Carl was either unemployed or on sabbatical for another four years. He did make the maximum contribution in all the other years which means he contributed for 37 out of the 39 years that are needed to qualify for a full pension. Since the maximum pension for new retirees in 2017 is $13,370, Carl's pension at age 65 would be about $12,700 a year plus future inflation-based increases. My advice to Carl is to hold off another five years before collecting this pension. That will be a tough sell!

By the way, if Carl had retired at 60 and started his CPP pension immediately, his contributory period would have been just 42 years instead of 47. The dropout period and the calculation of the maximum CPP pension would all be a little different, but it wouldn't change the basic idea that deferring CPP until 70 is a good idea.

Hanna receives a CPP pension as well, based on her own employment record. Her contributory period is shorter than 39 years because (a) she retired at 62 and (b) she can drop out the few years she stayed at home to raise the children. Offsetting these factors, Hanna also had more years of low or no contributions. The net effect is that her CPP entitlement is less than Carl's.

CPP Pension at a Later Starting Age

Assuming you stop working by age 65, the period after age 65 does not count when calculating the basic CPP pension. If Carl starts his CPP pension after 65, he will still get 95 percent of the maximum pension. In addition, he will get another 8.4 percent for every year that he waits beyond age 65. At age 70 then, the CPP pension would be increased by 42 percent plus the change in inflation between 65 and 70.

I should say it would be increased by *at least* 42 percent. If average wages in Canada rise faster than price inflation, it will increase by even more. Wages tend to grow faster than prices, at least in the long run. Wage inflation has outstripped price inflation in Canada since 1923 by an average of 1.37 percent a year. This wage–price differential is not guaranteed, of course. Some years it will be more than 1.37 percent and in other years it will be less. It can even be zero during a recession.

Let's be conservative and assume that the average differential is just 1 percent a year in future years. Doing the math, the CPP pension Carl would receive starting at age 70 would be 49.2 percent greater in real terms than if he starts payments at age 65. Instead of receiving $12,700 a year (in today's dollars), he would get $18,950 a year. Hanna's CPP pension at 70 would increase in a similar fashion.

One of the complications of starting CPP later is figuring out the survivor pension. If Carl died at age 68, for example, Hanna would be entitled to a survivor pension of as much as 60 percent of Carl's CPP pension. Unfortunately, this survivor benefit is capped. Hanna's own CPP pension plus the survivor benefit combined cannot exceed the maximum CPP payable to one person. The other complication is that the 60-percent survivor benefit is based on the maximum CPP pension payable to someone who is age 65. It is not adjusted for the 8.4-percent-per-year increase that Carl would have received for deferring his CPP start date. These quirks have been reflected in our calculations.

Impact of a Bigger CPP Pension

If Carl and Hanna wait until 70 to receive their CPP pension, they'll need to draw down their RRIF balance more rapidly between 65 and 70 to make up for the deferred CPP income. It is counter-intuitive, but in the long run their RRIF assets last longer if they do this. This is because the RRIF drawdowns slow down dramatically once they start their larger CPP pensions at age 70.

Figure 11.1 shows how this would look. Before age 70, the black bars represent only OAS pension, but by the time Carl is 73 and Hanna is 70, the black bars are much higher than they were in Figure 10.2 thanks to the bigger CPP pension.

Enhancement 2 greatly improves the overall financial situation for Carl and Hanna. They still run their RRIF and TFSA balances down to zero but not until age 86.

Figure 11.1: After Enhancement 2: Deferring CPP to 70

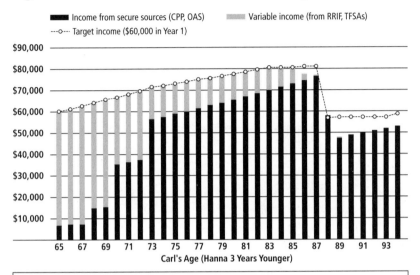

Legend: ■■■ Income from secure sources (CPP, OAS)   ▨▨▨ Variable income (from RRIF, TFSAs)   ---o--- Target income ($60,000 in Year 1)

Carl's Age (Hanna 3 Years Younger)

This is identical to Figure 10.2 (worst-case scenario) except Carl and Hanna defer CPP until age 70. The RRIF and TFSA assets now last until age 86 and the income gap in later years has shrunk.

Starting CPP later does more than just delay the time when their savings run dry. The more important metric is total income. Even in the later years when there is little or no RRIF income, the *total* income after Enhancement 2 is greater because so much more is coming from CPP. When Carl is 83, for example, total income is $30,000 greater than it was before Enhancement 2.

The benefits from Enhancement 2 don't stop there. Investment risk is significantly reduced because the savings that most expose the couple to risk have been drawn down earlier in their retirement and replaced by much more secure income in the form of a bigger CPP pension.

Longevity risk is also reduced because the portion of their overall income that is guaranteed for life is much greater. Even after Carl dies (at age 88), Hanna can look forward to receiving about $50,000 just from CPP and OAS alone. This is nearly $10,000 a year more than before Enhancement 2.

Enhancement 2 is so effective because it essentially transfers much of the retiree's investment risk and longevity risk back to the government, an entity that is much better equipped to deal with it than you are.

Common Objections to Deferring CPP

To an actuary who sees Figure 11.1 for the first time, Enhancement 2 represents a dream come true. It reduces the retiree's risk and increases the actuarial value of the pension at the same time. So why do so few retirees postpone their CPP until 70? Equally curious, why do so few financial planners endorse it? Based on the many comments from people who have read my articles on the subject in the *Globe and Mail* and the *National Post*, I think I know most of the reasons why the take-up rate is so low.

First, many people are not even aware they *can* defer CPP or how deferral can help them. When you are approaching age 65, the CPP administration office will send you an impressive package that outlines your CPP pension entitlement and asks you to complete an application form in order to start your CPP payments. The wording of the form practically assumes that you will choose to start your CPP pension by age 65. Besides, when you get an official-looking, personalized document from the government, the knee-jerk reaction is to follow instructions and send back the completed forms. This is especially true if it leads to you receiving money.

Second, we have a hard time envisioning a later starting age for our retirement benefits because society continues to reinforce the notion that age 65 is somehow magical. That used to be the age of mandatory retirement, the time when you could expect a gold watch and then be shown the door. Those days are gone, but the magic remains. Age 65 is when (a) you get into the movies for cheaper, (b) your prescription drugs are paid for by the government and (c) you can start to receive OAS pension. It is also the *latest* age that pensions from defined benefit pension plans from an employer can start (assuming you stopped working). For all of these intangible and somewhat irrelevant reasons, it is the age when you figure you should also be starting your CPP pension. Remember the response from my friend Hugh when he was asked why he was buying life insurance: "Isn't that what you are supposed to do?"

Third, many financial advisors encourage their clients to start their CPP pension as soon as possible and to hold off on spending their own savings. There is a cynical explanation for why advisors would give such advice and it stems from the fact that most advisors are remunerated based on a percentage of assets. Understandably, they would not want to see those assets dwindling too quickly! While I wouldn't want to assume this is what motivates them, you should at least be aware that your advisor's own compensation might be a factor.

I would like to think that most financial advisors genuinely try to do the best for their clients. If they are telling new retirees to start CPP early, it may be because they don't know that the real increase in CPP pension between ages 65 and 70 is closer to 50 percent rather than 42 percent, as was explained earlier. Similarly, most may not know that the **actuarial present value** of CPP pension starting at age 70 can be significantly greater.

Actuarial present value is how actuaries try to take into account all the information they have about a benefit and express it as a single number. That number represents the amount that would need to be set aside today to fund that benefit. It is basically a measure of overall value all captured in one number, just like a golfer's handicap.

Fourth, some people say they start their CPP pension early because they want to spend their money while they are still young. The logic of this escapes me because it seems to ignore the fact that money is fungible. In other words, money is money whether it comes in the form of CPP pension or a withdrawal from one's RRIF. I am not suggesting that retirees should spend less in their 60s, just that they get more of their income from sources other than the CPP.

Fifth, doubts about the long-term viability of the Canada Pension Plan still linger. Will CPP still be around when it comes time to collect? For someone who doesn't know how the governance of the CPP has evolved, this concern is at least a rational one. The CPP used to be funded on a pay-as-you go basis until 1997, which is not a stable way to fund a plan like this. In addition, some of the early investments made with CPP contributions were politically motivated and didn't inspire confidence that the best interests of the participants were being taken into account. For these reasons, it was understandable that people in the 1990s worried about the long-term sustainability of the plan.

Fortunately, major changes were made to how the CPP was run. Contribution rates were increased from 6 percent of covered pay in 1997 to 9.9 percent in 2003. This increase built up the fund assets and limited how much contributions would have to rise in the longer term. At the same time, an independent body (known as the **CPPIB**) was established to ensure that fund investments were based on sound principles instead of politics.

CPPIB stands for Canada Pension Plan Investment Board. This is one of the largest and most impressive investment institutions in the world, with large infrastructure investments extending around the globe.

In addition, the Chief Actuary of the Canada Pension Plan makes sophisticated long-term projections of demographics and assets, taking into account all the salient factors: investment returns, immigration, birth rates, employment rates, retirement ages, mortality rates and so on. These projections show that the current contribution rate is sustainable over the next 75 years and more. Even if a funding deficit developed, the contribution increase needed to pay for it would be small enough to be manageable. Politicians would almost certainly act to increase contributions rather than cut benefits. With such a sound governance structure in place, I have no worries about the future of the CPP.

By contrast, if you were an American and were relying on Social Security benefits in 20 years' time, I would say you have some reason to worry. US Social Security is funded on a pay-as-you-go basis, which requires ever-higher contributions as the working-age population matures and the number of retirees grows. Based on government projections of contributions and benefits, the amount of money left in the fund by 2034 will not be enough to make full payments. This is a real problem, given that Social Security does not have the legal right to borrow and American politicians do not seem to be able to bring themselves to increase taxes. It therefore seems the US Social Security system is on a collision course, but this doesn't affect the CPP.

The Real Reason for Not Postponing CPP

Perhaps the biggest reason for not starting CPP later is the "bird in the hand" argument. People tell me they don't want to postpone their CPP payments because they are afraid they might die early and not get full value from the Canada Pension Plan as a result. They hate the idea of leaving some of their money in the hands of the government upon death. That is why they prefer to start payments earlier, even if the actuarial value is lower.

This view is expressed so frequently and so forcefully that it deserves special attention. Allow me to point out the obvious: if you die early, you have bigger concerns than getting short-changed on your CPP pension (like not breathing!). Once you die, believe me, you are not going to be worried about missing out on CPP pension payments. Your bigger concern should be what happens if you live *longer* than you expected because you will still be around to regret a bad decision!

You might counter by saying that your concerns about early death are altruistic. You want to be sure that the loved ones you are leaving behind are well taken care of. The trouble with this argument is that starting CPP early does more harm than good as far as the surviving spouse is concerned.

This last point is a curious one. You would think, for example, that Hanna would be better off financially in widowhood considering she would not have to share the remaining RRIF assets. The problem, though, is that Carl's death shrinks or eliminates the government pensions he was receiving. The value of those lost government benefits more than offsets the remaining RRIF assets that Carl would have consumed.

Fair enough, but let's test this argument and see how well Hanna is protected if Carl dies at age 75 instead of 88. This scenario is captured in Figure 11.2. The result is not perfect, but if Carl dies at 75, Hanna is in a slightly better financial position if she and Carl had started their CPP pensions at 70 instead of 65. By deferring CPP to 70, Hanna's total income is indeed lower at ages 79 to 81, but then it is higher every year after that, no matter how long she lives.*

Figure 11.2: Deferring CPP Benefits Hanna Even if Carl Dies at a Younger Age

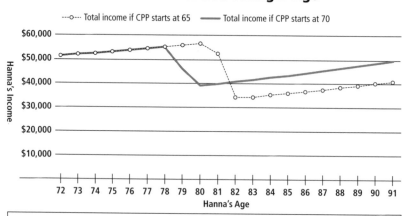

This is based on the same data as Figure 11.1 except Carl dies at 75 (when Hanna is 72). Deferring CPP to age 70 means Hanna has less income between ages 79 and 81 but more after that.

It gets even stranger. From Hanna's perspective, her long-term financial situation is less secure if Carl died in his 70s rather than in his late 60s. If he died at, say, 67, then the 60-percent survivor benefit

---

* Income is lower at ages 79 to 81 because RRIF assets have run out more quickly under Enhancement 2. By age 82, the RRIF balance is nil even without Enhancement 2, and the bigger CPP under Enhancement 2 produces more overall income.

from Carl's CPP pension would at least be payable for the next three years, at which point Hanna's deferred CPP pension kicks in. If Carl died at 75, though, Hanna's survivor benefit payable would be less because of the restrictions on how much pension an individual can receive under the CPP.

Other Objections to Deferring CPP Benefits

Having shot holes in the primary reasons people give for not starting CPP at 70, I will concede that situations exist when it is better to start your CPP pension early. In particular, you may not have enough assets to tide you over until age 70. In the most extreme case, consider a couple who have both earned close to the maximum CPP pension by age 60. For the two of them combined, the amount payable from age 60 would be about $18,000 a year. If they were to defer their CPP payments until age 70, they would need about $180,000 in savings to provide an equivalent amount of income in the interim. If they don't have that much in savings, then postponing CPP will obviously not work. Enhancement 2 is a strategy for people with significant savings, preferably north of $200,000 in the case of couples and about half that amount in the case of single persons.

Another good reason for starting CPP earlier is if you have a shorter-than-average life expectancy, although this would have to be true of both you and your spouse. As we saw in the above example where Carl dies at 75, Hanna is still better off if she and Carl both wait until 70 to collect CPP.

A third possible reason not to defer CPP is if you retired at or before age 60 and had many years of low or no contributions before then. If you defer CPP until 65 or later, you are adding another five years of no contributions. Because of the way the benefit is calculated, you might not receive a big enough increase in CPP pension to make deferral worthwhile.

Fourth, the advantages of deferring CPP are blunted considerably if you keep on working beyond age 65. This phenomenon is explained in Chapter 19.

Finally, you might find yourself unable to wait until 70 for emotional reasons. If you are like many people, your sense of self-worth is intertwined with your financial worth. For most of your working life, you were saving so as to improve your financial situation. It would have been a comfort to watch your RRSP account balance growing steadily. Drawing down personal assets in retirement is hard to do because it is a grim reminder not only of our dwindling influence in this life but also of our own mortality. Drawing down our assets *more quickly*, as we would have to do under Enhancement 2, compounds the difficulty. This explains why people might be *reluctant* to adopt Enhancement 2, but it is not a good reason to reject it.

Why Not Defer OAS, Too?

If starting one's CPP pension at age 70 is such a good idea, then why not start OAS pension at 70 as well? Many people don't realize it, but you do have the option of deferring OAS commencement until 70. There are a couple of reasons why I am reluctant to recommend doing it, though.

First, the actuarial adjustment you receive is much less than it is for CPP. In the case of OAS, the increase at age 70 versus 65 is only 36 percent. The second reason is that starting CPP late is already forcing the average retiree to draw down their RRIF balance much faster than they bargained on doing. It is a good move, but it's one that makes people uncomfortable. Asking people to start OAS late as well will accelerate the RRIF drawdown and make people just that much more uncomfortable. By the way, I make an exception for really high earners who would see their entire OAS pension clawed back anyway. They might as well postpone the start date until 70 because they won't receive any value from OAS before then.

Takeaways

1. Enhancement 2 entails postponing the start of your CPP pension until 70.

2. By doing so, CPP income is increased by nearly 50 percent in the case of someone who contributed to CPP until age 65. This increased pension is inflation-protected and payable for life.

3. Under Enhancement 2, you are essentially transferring some of your investment risk and longevity risk back to the government, and you are doing so at zero cost.

4. In spite of these advantages, very few Canadians postpone their CPP until 70. There are many plausible reasons why they reject this option but few good reasons for those who have the financial means to wait until 70 to collect their CPP.

5. You need substantial savings to be able to adopt Enhancement 2. In the case of a couple, it is roughly $200,000.

12

ENHANCEMENT 3
BUYING AN ANNUITY

Maybe it was a mistake to include the word "annuity" in the title of this chapter. For a variety of reasons, annuities are not popular, even though they help to ensure you will never outlive your money.

Remember, the primary purpose of a decumulation strategy is to reach your income target. In the case of Carl and Hanna, the first two enhancements went a long way to achieving this goal. Still, they do not have total financial security yet.

We need to find some more income for Carl and Hanna—especially for Hanna if Carl dies early. It's time to see whether Enhancement 3 can help. Under this enhancement, we will assume that Carl and Hanna use some of their RRIF assets at the point of retirement to purchase an annuity. They allocate 30 percent of their RRIF—an amount equal to $150,000—for the annuity purchase. This leaves them with $350,000 in their RRIF.

The type of annuity they should buy is one that is payable as long as either one of them is still alive—what actuaries call a "joint and survivor annuity." Given Carl and Hanna's overall financial position, the survivor pension should be 60 to 75 percent of what is payable when both of them are alive.

An annuity that continues at 100 percent to the surviving spouse would have some appeal for Carl and Hanna. It would provide better income protection for Hanna if Carl were to die sometime in his 70s, the most vulnerable decade, as it turns out, based on my spreadsheet calculations. That protection comes at a high price, though, since a 100-percent survivor benefit is expensive. It might be better to settle for a 60- or 75-percent survivor benefit and buy some term life insurance instead; at least for the period when Hanna's survivor income is most at risk.

Another question is whether to buy an **indexed annuity**. I recommend against it. Insurance companies don't like to sell indexed annuities and most people don't like to buy one. As a result, indexed annuities tend to be over-priced, if and when you do find one. Equally important, an indexed annuity is not necessary because the income target at later ages is rising more slowly than inflation. And remember that both CPP and OAS are fully indexed to inflation, so there is some inflation protection in any event.

An **indexed annuity** is an annuity that provides inflation protection. It increases annually in line with increases in the general inflation rate. Such an annuity will be much more expensive than a regular annuity wherein the payments are the same every year.

At present interest rates, a single premium of $150,000 buys about $8,250 of annuity income with two-thirds of that amount continuing to Hanna if Carl dies first. If the annuity reduces on either person's death—which is unusual but not a bad idea—the amount would be a little higher. Given the cost, $8,250 of annuity income may not sound like much, but let's see how the annuity purchase would affect Carl and Hanna before deciding against it.

Impact of Enhancement 3

Enhancement 3 is reflected in Figure 12.1, which also includes the previous two enhancements. By purchasing the annuity, their RRIF produces 30 percent less income because it is 30 percent smaller. Nevertheless, the annuity purchase helps to put Carl and Hanna over the top. If you compare Figures 11.1 and 12.1, you will see that the income gap that existed when Carl was 86 (and Hanna 83) or older has been closed. They achieve their income target for their entire lives. This is true even if Hanna lives past 100.

Figure 12.1: After Annuity Purchase

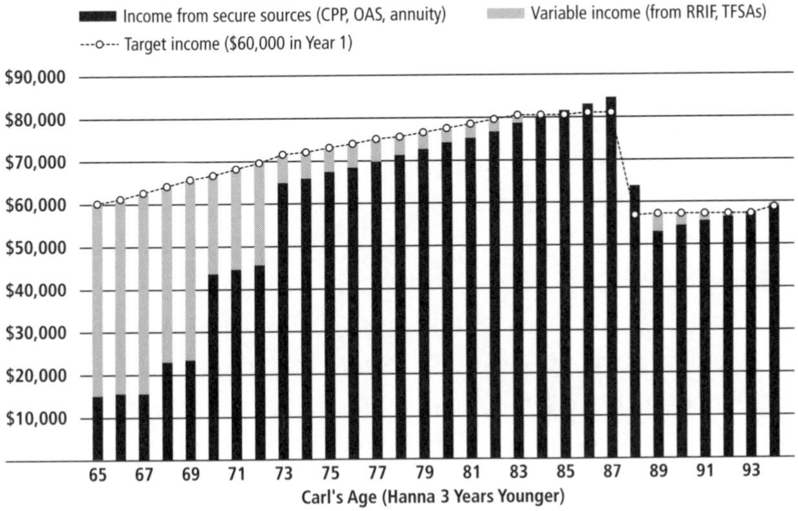

This is identical to Figure 11.1 except that Carl and Hanna use 30% of their RRIF assets at retirement to buy an annuity. The income gap is now closed.

Enhancements 2 and 3 have another advantage that doesn't really jump out from the chart. By the time Carl is age 80 or so, those enhancements virtually eliminate whatever income uncertainty Carl and Hanna still have. By 80, the bars in Figure 12.1 are almost all solid black (instead of grey), which means that their income is totally secure. This makes them virtually immune from both investment risk and longevity risk.

This result is possible because Carl and Hanna got rid of their risky assets first, meaning their RRIF. They started this process with Enhancement 2 by drawing down their RRIF assets more aggressively in their 60s. Enhancement 3 continued the process as they directed 30 percent of their RRIF balance toward the purchase of an annuity. This transformed more of their riskier RRIF assets into a safe and sure income stream in the form of an annuity.

While drawing down their RRIF by their early 70s might make them feel a little panicky, they need to remember that it is part of the plan. Carl and Hanna have passed along most of the risk to an insurance company and the government—and they are better off as a result.

Convinced Yet?

Perhaps you still have a lingering distrust or distaste for annuities. You may find the charts intriguing but may be wondering whether you're missing something. Surely there must be a reason why fewer than 5 percent of all people who are in a position to buy an annuity actually do so.

Well, you do lose something by buying an annuity with 30 percent of your assets: you lose 30 percent of the upside potential if the RRIF assets achieve better-than-average returns. However, this lost potential, which is known as opportunity cost, is not as punitive as it sounds. As the next example will show, the lost opportunity for a higher benefit is something you did not need in the first place and certainly were never counting on. This harkens back to the earlier comments I made about the diminishing utility of money.

So far, I have been showing investment results under a worst-case scenario. That's because it is important to be prepared for the worst even when one hopes for the best. What if Carl and Hanna enjoyed at least average returns? If we go back to Chapter 7, Figure 7.1 showed the range of returns one could expect with a 50-50 asset mix over various time periods. Instead of assuming returns at the bottom of each range, as we have up until now, let's assume median investment returns.

The result is shown in Figure 12.2, which compares two scenarios: one in which Carl and Hanna adopt the first two enhancements but not the annuity purchase, and the other in which they also buy an annuity. When investment returns are at the median (neither high nor low), the total amount of income is virtually the same whether Carl and Hanna buy an annuity or draw income from the RRIF. Even then, the annuity is still a better bet because it will continue to be paid in the event that Carl or Hanna live beyond age 95.

Figure 12.2: Income with Median Investment Returns

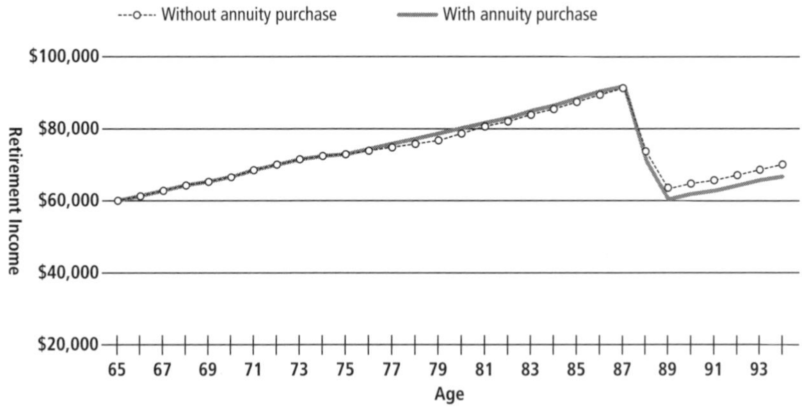

This is like Figure 12.1 but with median returns. Results assuming annuity purchase are about the same, but with less risk.

The RRIF outperforms the annuity only when investments do *very* well, meaning better than the median. But in this case, Carl and Hanna will have much more income than their income target in any event, whether they buy the annuity or not.

The analysis takes us to only one conclusion: Buying the annuity provides better protection when Carl and Hanna really need it, which is when their investment returns are poor. They give up nothing if future investment returns turn out to be closer to the median. They give something up only if investment returns turn out to be very high, but what they lose in that case is something they weren't counting on and can easily do without. Enhancement 3 is, therefore, a keeper.

There is always an exception. Actually, there are two. Carl and Hanna should probably take a pass on the annuity if they *both* have a shorter life expectancy than the average. This is the same conclusion we reached when we analyzed whether or not to defer CPP pension until age 70. The other potential problem is if the marriage is not entirely solid. Buying a joint and survivor annuity ties your fate to that of your spouse for the rest of time. It's great if you have a solid marriage but maybe not so great otherwise.

Buying an Annuity Later

The case for annuities is quite persuasive if you focus on what happens in a worst-case investment scenario. Not everyone does their retirement planning based on a worst-case investment scenario, though; and we have seen that if investment returns track the median, the merits of buying an annuity in one's 60s are less obvious.

However, like wine, annuities get better with age. This is because of something called a **mortality credit**. The mortality credit is there no matter when you buy the annuity, but it is worth a lot more if you buy it at age 75 than at age 65. This is because the probability of death at 75 is much greater. I'll provide an example to show how beneficial it can be to buy an annuity in one's 70s instead of at the point of retirement.

Annuities pay as much income as they do because insurance companies have many annuitants in their pool and each year some of them will die. The insurance company will take this fact into account when they price the annuity. The surviving annuitants benefit by virtue of getting a higher income than if everyone was assumed to die at a ripe old age. This bump in income is the **mortality credit**.

Assume Hanna is now 75 and is now a widow. She has $100,000 in her RRIF and needs to decide whether to draw an income with that money or purchase an annuity. An annuity with payments guaranteed for five years would provide Hanna with annual income of $8,600. This would be payable no matter how long she lives.

As for the income from the RRIF, we can already guess that it would underperform the annuity if future investment returns are terrible. But what about if Hanna achieved median investment returns? In that case, Hanna could withdraw about $7,200 a year from her RRIF until age 95 when the account would be exhausted. In other words, Hanna would get $1,400 a year less income with the RRIF and would have no protection from the risk of outliving her money.

If you are still not sold on the annuity (at least at age 75), it might be because you have one or more of the following qualms. First, you might say that the annuity would provide a much smaller death benefit if Hanna died shortly after it started. That is true, but the question for Hanna is, how important is it to provide death benefits given that she is a widow?

A second potential objection is that she is unlikely to live until 95. While 95 is pushing the longevity envelope a little, Hanna's actual life expectancy, as measured from age 75, is really not much less than 95. And, of course, she might live until 100.

A third potential objection is that her investments might do better than the median. On the other hand, there is an equal chance that they will do worse.

Finally, what if Hanna needs some emergency funds? The annuity wouldn't provide enough flexibility.

All of these objections are good reasons to leave some money in the RRIF (such as 25 or 50 percent, depending on one's needs), but the case for using perhaps half of one's remaining RRIF assets to buy an annuity at age 75 or so is still a strong one.

In summary, buying an annuity at the point of retirement with about 30 percent of your RRIF assets is advisable. Whether you do this or not, it probably makes sense to buy another annuity when you turn 75 or so in order to take advantage of the mortality credit.

If buying an annuity at 75 is better than doing so at age 65, then why not wait until you're 80? The trouble is that the longer you wait, the less likely you are to do it. By age 80, your adult children may very well try to stop you from proceeding with an annuity purchase. And, of course, you are exposing yourself to a painful market correction the longer you wait.

Lingering Doubts

Dealing with qualms about annuities is a little like being the hero in a zombie movie. Just when I think I've done away with the problem, it somehow keeps on getting up again. Very briefly, here are a few more common reasons why people decide to reject annuities and why they should reconsider:

> **"I can do better if the money is fully invested in the markets."** If you are risk-averse, the only scenario that really counts is when investment returns are worse than normal. That is when you need protection. Under this scenario, you definitely cannot do better on your own.

> **"Interest rates are very low these days, which means the current cost of an annuity is unusually high."** This is absolutely true and it would be nice if interest rates were higher. On the other hand, the results given earlier in this chapter fully build in these low rates and we found that buying an annuity is still a better choice than not buying one. You could take a chance and wait a few years, but (a) rates may not turn higher or (b) you might get hit with bad investment returns in the meantime—the very thing you were trying to avoid.

> **"If it's such a great idea, why isn't my financial advisor suggesting an annuity?"** Some financial advisors do recommend the purchase of an annuity. And when they do, their clients generally follow their advice. As for the advisors who don't mention annuities, their views might be subconsciously influenced by the fact that they want their own income stream to be steady or growing. Buying an annuity gives the advisor a one-time commission, but the advisor's future remuneration will diminish.

> **"The insurance companies don't treat you fairly. It is better not to deal with them."** Behavioural economists Daniel Kahneman

and Amos Tversky conducted an interesting experiment back in the 1980s. In the experiment, Subject A is given a bag with $100 in it and is told he can keep the money, but only if he can reach an agreement with Subject B to share it. If both subjects were totally rational beings, then Subject B should be happy to get just $1; after all, that would be a total windfall. Subject A could then keep the other $99. While this may be how economists (and actuaries) would behave, it is not the way most normal people think. In the experiment, Subject A had to share between 30 percent and 50 percent of the $100 in order to make a deal with Subject B.

This experiment provides another insight into why most of us prefer not to deal with insurance companies: Just like Subject B, we don't want to be pushed around. Are insurance companies unfair? This is debatable, but it certainly is the widely held perception. The insurers have all the information while we, the consumers, have almost none. There is no transparency in the profits and expenses they build into products like annuities, and this might lead one to think they are being unfair in how they deal with us.

In spite of any qualms you may have, are you really prepared to take a pass on a better decumulation strategy as a result? The only important question is whether or not you are better off buying an annuity, and the examples in this chapter suggest you are.

Takeaways

1. Unless you have a very large amount of savings, at least 60 percent of the annuity you buy should continue to be paid to the surviving spouse. This measure makes up for the loss of the deceased spouse's CPP and OAS income.

2. It is better to buy a non-indexed annuity.

3. Buying an annuity upon your retirement with about 30 percent of your RRIF assets will ensure you have more retirement income in the event that future investment returns are truly bad.

4. Survivor benefits in the event of a spouse's early death also tend to be a little better if you buy an annuity than if you do not.

5. There is an opportunity cost to buying an annuity: you will not have as big a windfall within your RRIF if investments do really well, although you will still have more income than you had expected.

6. Whether you buy an annuity at retirement or not, you should consider buying another annuity around age 75 if you still have substantial tax-sheltered assets then.

13

FINE-TUNING THE ASSET MIX

So far, we haven't paid much attention to the asset mix of the RRIF investments. The major takeaway from Chapter 7 (Investment Risk) was that you need to invest in stocks to have any chance of a decent return. But just how much of your portfolio should be in stocks? A 50-50 mix (50 percent in stocks and 50 percent in bonds) doesn't seem too bad, judging from the results that Carl and Hanna have achieved with the first three enhancements. But can we do better?

There wasn't a lot of science involved in picking the 50-50 asset mix. I had Carl and Hanna go with 50-50 for a few vague and, admittedly, flimsy reasons. It is more conservative than 60-40, which professional pension fund managers have seen fit to maintain for decades. The greater conservatism seems appropriate, as retirees are more risk-averse than the sponsors of a large pension plan. On the other hand, it is a little *less* conservative than the asset mix within comparable **target date funds (TDFs),** and that may or may not be appropriate.

A **target date fund (TDF)** is a balanced fund that is targeted to investors whose retirement falls in a certain range of years, such as 2018 to 2022; the closer the retirement date, the lower the weighting in stocks. The idea is that older retirees should be facing less risk. The typical asset mix in a TDF meant for imminent retirees is 40-60.

While it seems that a 50-50 mix cannot be too far off the mark, it is time to investigate whether a different mix might provide a better trade-off between risk and return. The starting point is to assume that Carl and Hanna have already implemented the first three enhancements. If they have indeed done this, then their asset mix is not really 50-50. That's because the annuity purchase (Enhancement 3) quietly changed the mix. Let me explain how.

An annuity is really just another investment. And as an investment, it behaves very much like a long-term bond, meaning that the value rises when bond yields fall, and vice versa. As bonds go, an annuity is super safe because the return is fixed for life, so you don't have to worry about reinvesting it down the road the way you would with a regular bond investment.

Since the annuity purchase price in Chapter 12 was $150,000, the annuity effectively reduced the overall stock weighting from 50 percent to 37.5 percent and increased the bond weighting to 62.5 percent. This is described in Table 13.1 (To keep it simple, I am ignoring the TFSA.)

Table 13.1: How Enhancement 3 Changed the Asset Mix

	Before Buying an Annuity	After Buying an Annuity
Assets in stocks in the RRIF	$250,000	$175,000
Assets in bonds in the RRIF	$250,000	$175,000
Assets in the annuity	Nil	$150,000
Total assets	$500,000	$500,000
Effective asset mix (stocks/bonds*)	50-50	37.5-62.5

*The annuity is classified as a bond for this purpose.

To restore the 50-50 mix, we need to sell $75,000 worth of bonds in the RRIF and put the money in stocks. This brings the holdings in the RRIF back up to $250,000 in stocks while the bonds are reduced to $100,000.

If you consider the RRIF assets in isolation, it looks like we changed the asset mix to 71-29, but the *overall* mix is 50-50 when you include the annuity. This is shown in Table 13.2.

Table 13.2: Restoring a 50-50 Asset Mix to the Retirement Portfolio

	Before Rebalancing	After Rebalancing
Assets in stocks in the RRIF	$175,000	$250,000
Assets in bonds in the RRIF	$175,000	$100,000
Assets in the annuity	$150,000	$150,000
Total assets including annuity	$500,000	$500,000
Asset mix within the RRIF (stocks/bonds)	50-50	71-29
Overall asset mix	37.5-62.5	50-50

Going from a mix of 50-50 to 71-29 within the RRIF is a major change. You would be hard-pressed to find any pension fund in Canada with 71 percent of its assets in stocks, as it would be considered too risky. If Carl and Hanna make that change and incur the worst-case investment scenario, you would think the results would be much worse than with a 50-50 mix. Surprisingly, this is not the case. The result is shown in Figure 13.1.

If you're wondering whether you've seen this chart before, you have, sort of. It looks strikingly similar to Figure 12.1 from the previous chapter. Even though the asset mix of the RRIF was changed dramatically (from 50-50 to 71-29), it barely affected retirement income. This outcome hardly seems possible. Investment experts are in near-universal agreement that the most important factor in investing is getting the asset mix right, and yet here we find that a major change in mix barely makes a difference.

One reason is that the RRIF assets have shrunk considerably by age 70, as Enhancements 2 and 3 accelerated the drawdown of the RRIF. As a result, the RRIF plays only a minor role in determining overall income. (You will remember that this shrinking of the RRIF was intentional because it minimizes the one source of retirement income that is unpredictable.)

Figure 13.1: All 3 Enhancements Plus High Equity Weighting

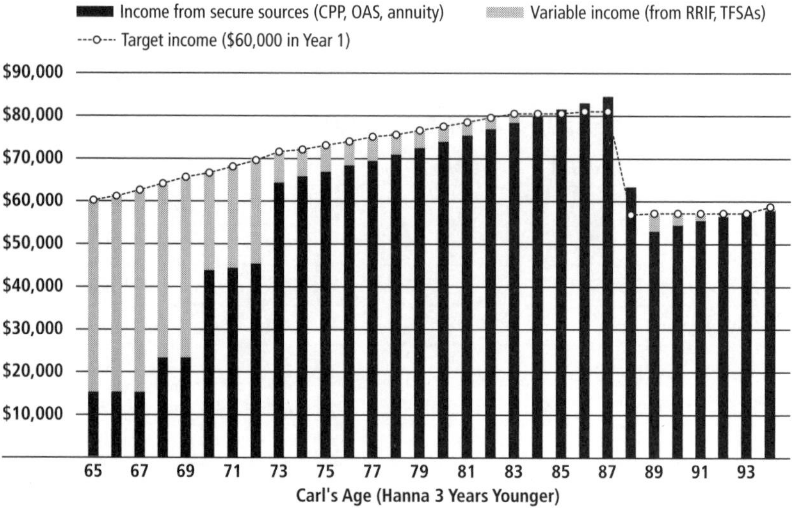
Income from secure sources (CPP, OAS, annuity)
Variable income (from RRIF, TFSAs)
Target income ($60,000 in Year 1)
$90,000
$80,000
$70,000
$60,000
$50,000
$40,000
$30,000
$20,000
$10,000
65 67 69 71 73 75 77 79 81 83 85 87 89 91 93
Carl's Age (Hanna 3 Years Younger)

This is identical to Figure 12.1 (worst-case scenario) except the stock weighting in the RRIF mix has been increased from 50% to 71%.

Another reason is that we are comparing the two asset mixes only under the worst-case investment scenario. As it turns out, expected returns on this scenario are not much different whether one is invested in stocks or in bonds. This is either a quirk of the Monte Carlo simulation we used to establish the worst-case scenario or it is a reflection of the peculiar times we live in. Usually a worst-case result for stocks should be much worse than it is for bonds, but the fact that interest rates have sunk so low in recent years has increased the downside potential of bonds. Any significant rise in bond yields will create a major capital loss.

If Carl and Hanna experience *median* investment returns instead, the 71-29 asset mix produces slightly more income than the 50-50 mix does—a result that is more in line with what you would normally expect. As for the best-case investment scenario, the results are much better with the 71-29 mix. This is all summarized in Table 13.3.

**Table 13.3: RRIF Results Using a 71-29 Asset
          Mix Instead of 50-50**

Worst-case scenario	Same or slightly worse
Median scenario	Slightly better
Best-case scenario	Much better

Stocks Are the Place to Be

What does all this tell you? First, it means that Carl and Hanna should
be reasonably comfortable with a 70-30 asset mix for their RRIF in
spite of the fact that they are about to retire. If they had complete faith
in the Monte Carlo simulation that produced this result, then they
should be *really* comfortable with a 70-30 mix. This is, of course, at
odds with any advice you will get from financial advisors, but keep in
mind that the annuity acts like an investment in bonds.

If you are at all skeptical of whether the Monte Carlo simulation
process truly simulates reality (and who isn't?), then maybe you dial
the equity weighting down to 60 percent instead of 70 percent. You
will have the comfort of knowing that a 60-40 mix is similar to what
pension fund managers have been using for eons. If you are 65 or
younger, I don't see any good reason to adopt a stock weighting as
low as 50 percent in your RRIF or RRSP, apart from wanting to avoid
a lecture from your financial planner.

This isn't to say that the future is going to be rosy for stocks.
There could be a correction or even a bear market that lasts for years.
What the Monte Carlo simulation indicates is that bond returns won't
be much better and could easily be worse.

The second conclusion is that once you decide on your asset mix,
you may as well not change it before age 70. This will seem contrary
to the usual financial planning advice, but keep in mind that between
ages 65 and 70, the RRIF assets diminish significantly because of
Enhancement 2. As a result, the overall weighting in stocks drops automatically. This is shown in Table 13.4, which shows how the overall

asset mix for Carl and Hanna changes between 65 and 70 even if the asset mix in the RRIF alone is a constant 60-40. A 60-40 mix in the RRIF at age 65 translates into an overall asset mix of 42-58, and by age 70 it becomes 37-63. This is why there is little reason to worry about being too heavily weighted in stocks.

Table 13.4: How the Overall Asset Mix Changes by Age 70*

	Mix at 65	Mix at 70
Assets in stocks in the RRIF	$210,000	$126,000
Assets in bonds in the RRIF	$140,000	$84,000
Total assets in the RRIF	$350,000	$210,000
RRIF asset mix	60-40	60-40
Assets in the annuity**	$150,000	$130,000
Total assets	$500,000	$340,000
Effective weighting in stocks	42%	37%

* This assumes that investment returns are at the median, as derived by the Monte Carlo simulation.
** The estimated actuarial value of the remaining annuity payments.

Table 13.4 may be a little shocking for another reason. Of the $500,000 in RRIF assets that Carl and Hanna started with, $150,000 was used to buy the annuity. As for the remaining $350,000, it shrank to just $210,000 by age 70 because the RRIF was paying out more as a result of deferring CPP. And this is assuming a median investment return. If Carl and Hanna had experienced the worst-case investment scenario, the RRIF balance at 70 would have shrunk down to just $103,000.

This type of situation can test your resolve. You need to have a lot of faith that your decumulation strategy is on track when you see your RRIF assets dropping like a rock. You will have to remind yourself that, however much your RRIF assets shrink by accelerating the drawdown, you more than made up for that loss with a bigger CPP pension plus the income from the annuity.

The third finding from this analysis is to make sure you are using your financial advisor effectively. If all the planner is doing is helping you set your asset mix, the exercise is practically a waste of time in this unusual environment of prolonged low interest rates (what the industry refers to as "low for long"). You could choose a 60-40 mix for the RRIF and take comfort in the knowledge that you will not be too far off. It might be a little too conservative, if anything. We will assume that Carl and Hanna use a 60-40 mix for the remaining scenarios in this book.

It would seem that fine-tuning the asset mix is a failed experiment. It doesn't do much to increase income or reduce risk, but at least this exercise yielded some new insights into setting the asset mix and provided some justification for upping the stock weighting in the RRIF.

Takeaways

1. When assessing your asset mix in retirement, remember to include the value of the annuity as part of your overall portfolio and consider it equivalent to investing in bonds.

2. If you want an overall asset mix of 50-50, you may want to increase the stock weighting in the RRIF to 70 percent. To get to an overall mix of 40-60, the asset mix in the RRIF should be about 60-40.

3. Under a worst-case investment scenario, there is little difference in outcome whether the RRIF has a 50-50 or a 70-30 asset mix. A mix of 70-30 produces a slightly better result if you enjoy a median return and a much better result if returns are well above average.

4. As the RRIF assets get drawn down between ages 65 and 70, the stock weighting in the overall portfolio will automatically shrink. You may, therefore, not want to reduce the stock weighting in your RRIF before age 70.

14

DID YOU SAVE ENOUGH?

We have not yet finished mapping out the possible enhancements to the decumulation strategy, but this is a good time to hit the pause button. The first three enhancements almost always make sense, assuming you have enough savings to carry them out, but they don't answer one important question: With a given level of savings, how much income can you draw?

This question reminds me of a scene from the 1990s sitcom *That '70s Show*. Even though he didn't have the slightest aptitude as a salesman, Red Forman (the prickly father played brilliantly by Kurtwood Smith) gets a job selling appliances in his neighbour's store. In the scene, a lady comes into the store to buy a refrigerator. Red tries to figure out what she wants, but they just don't speak the same language. He asks her, "How many cubic feet of food does your family consume in a week?" Not surprisingly, the lady cannot answer that question and eventually walks away without buying anything.

I'm not going to ask you how many cubic feet of money you will consume in retirement, although I will ask you to think about how safe you want your income to be.

You might be just a little suspicious of how neatly things have been working out for Carl and Hanna. Without a good decumulation strategy, their $550,000 in savings (including $50,000 in TFSAs) was nowhere close to producing the retirement income they thought they needed. But then they adopted three enhancements and voila, $550,000 was just enough, even if Carl and Hanna both live to a ripe old age and experience very poor investment returns.

If you think this is all just a little too tidy, you'd be right. I just felt it was useful to start with the simple case before addressing the question posed at the beginning of this chapter: Did you save enough? We are now in a position to tackle this question. Then we can resume the rollout of the enhancements.

No Simple Rule of Thumb

In the case of Carl and Hanna, their $550,000 in savings turned out to be enough to generate $60,000 of income under most economic scenarios.* But how could they have known that in advance?

Ideally there would be a simple rule of thumb to tell retirees how much can be produced with a given level of savings. The trouble is, the target depends on too many variables, including retirement age, marital status, the taxability of savings and the amount of CPP pension payable. The percentage of RRIF assets you use to buy an annuity is also an important factor. It should usually be 30 percent, but sometimes retirees don't have enough savings to buy an annuity at all. Finally, interest rates and stock market expectations change over time, so the right answer today might not still hold true a year or two from now.

Defining the Income Range

If I can't tell you definitively how much retirement income your savings can generate, I can at least define a range. As we will see, this

---

* All references to income target in this chapter are to the first year of retirement. Spending in subsequent years is assumed to climb based on the spending pattern identified in Chapter 4.

range will change over time, which is fine as long as you have a way to stay abreast of those changes.

The top end of the range is the "best-estimate target." This is the amount of retirement income you can generate under so-called normal conditions, which include a median rate of return on investments and an average lifespan. By definition, you will have a 50-percent chance that the income under a best-estimate set of assumptions will last a lifetime. The bottom end of the range is what I call the "safe target." This is the amount of retirement income that you will be able to generate for the rest of your life under 99 percent of all possible scenarios.

Alas, you can never be 100-percent safe. The other 1 percent of scenarios includes dying at an extreme age or struggling with investment returns that are even worse than my so-called worst-case scenario. And I'm not even taking into account the prospect of certain rainy day events that can disrupt the best-laid plans.

It is time for a confession: we actuaries can't resist building in some cushion—what we call Provision for Adverse Deviation or PfAD. In this case, I suggest calculating both the best-estimate income target and the safe target on the assumption that you will still want some money left over at the end of your expected lifetime. Why? Well, you might live longer than that, for one thing. Also, you will want to leave a little money behind for your executors to settle your estate as well as leaving some money to loved ones (other than your spouse, who is already being taken care of).

The size of cushion I am suggesting in this case is 10 percent of the savings you had at the point of retirement. In the case of Carl and Hanna, that would be $55,000 (10 percent of both the RRIF and the TFSA in Year 1). The 10-percent figure is totally arbitrary, of course. Super-savers and Cleavers will want that cushion to be bigger, and YOLOs will want it to be smaller. I would point out that it is actually not that large in any case, since it doesn't reflect inflation over the course of retirement.

We don't have to build in another cushion for rainy day events because we have already done that. In the case of Carl and Hanna, I assumed they would be setting aside 5 percent of their retirement income each year until age 80 so they could pay for medium-sized emergencies. I did not factor in the more serious spending shocks. For instance, Hanna might eventually need a very expensive drug that's not covered by her provincial drug program. Or Carl and Hanna might get divorced. Or one of them might require long-term care for a prolonged period. Life does not lend itself easily to absolute certainty.

This brings to mind a Boston College survey that was reported in *The Atlantic* magazine in April 2011. The survey covered 165 wealthy households, each with at least $25 million in investable assets. The average net worth was $78 million. When asked how much money they would need to feel financially secure, the average response was 25 percent *more* than what they already had! It seems no amount of money will ever vanquish anxiety. The best prescription I can offer is to increase the amount of income you receive from secure sources. Increasing your financial knowledge is also useful, which I suppose is why you are reading this book in the first place.

Income You Can Expect from Savings

With these thoughts in mind, Table 14.1 shows how much income a couple can generate from a given amount of savings. The income is inflation-adjusted after retirement based on the spending pattern that was described in Chapter 4.

A critically important assumption in estimating total income is the amount of income that will come in the form of CPP pension. For the purposes of Table 14.1, I have assumed that the couple's combined CPP pension at age 65 is 65 percent more than the maximum for one person.* For instance, one spouse might have 90 percent of the maximum CPP pension and the other spouse would have 75 percent. The other assumption in Table 14.1 is that, at 65, the couple has $1 in TFSA savings for every $10 in RRIF savings.

---

* This also happens to be what we assumed for Carl and Hanna.

Table 14.1: Income from a Given Amount of Savings*

Savings at retirement	Safe Income Target	Best-Estimate Income Target
$330,000	$47,000	$52,300
$550,000	$59,000	$67,000
$880,000	$71,400	$82,500
$1,320,000	$87,300	$105,600
$2,200,000	$118,100	$151,000

*Including income from CPP, OAS and any annuity

One of the remarkable things about Table 14.1 is the tightness of the ranges. The safe income target is not that much less than the best-estimate target. This is because the CPP pension was optimized by deferring payment until 70 and also because 30 percent of the RRIF assets at 65 was used to purchase an annuity. These enhancements eliminated a great deal of uncertainty at what I consider to be a reasonable cost. This, of course, is exactly what a good decumulation strategy should do.

The Income Range and the Acceptable Income Zone

This is a good place to draw a comparison between the income range I have outlined above and the acceptable income zone that was first described in Chapter 3. In an ideal world, the income range and the acceptable zone would be identical. Unfortunately, there is no way to guarantee this, as it depends so much on the level of savings you have when you retire. What this book attempts to do is raise the income range as much as possible.

Single Retirees

So far, I have virtually ignored the situation of the single retiree. For any given level of savings, the single retiree will not be able to produce nearly as much income as a couple. This is because the single person has only one CPP pension and one OAS pension. On the other hand, the single person shouldn't need as much income.

Table 14.2 shows the safe income target and the best-estimate target at different levels of savings for a single woman at age 65. (For a single man, the amounts of income would be a little higher because the life expectancy for men is two to three years shorter.)

Table 14.2: Income Target for a 65-Year-Old Single Retiree (Female)

Savings at 65	Safe Income Target	Best-Estimate Income Target
$220,000*	$29,500	$32,900
$440,000*	$36,800	$44,800
$660,000	$53,600	$56,700
$990,000	$63,900	$74,500
$1,540,000	$71,000	$104,200

*Annuity is purchased with just 20% of savings instead of 30%.

The targets for the single retiree were based on that individual being entitled to 90 percent of the maximum CPP pension at age 65. Death occurred at 95 for purposes of the safe target and 92 for the best-estimate target (which is a little conservative). The other assumptions that were used to produce Tables 14.1 and 14.2 are summarized in Appendix C.

What About Your Own Income Target?

The above tables are for illustrative purposes only. It is highly unlikely that the reader will be able to use the tables directly, nor is that the intention. I have enlisted the help of the IT people at Morneau Shepell to develop an online calculator that you can use to determine your specific safe income target and best-estimate target. This tool is described in the next chapter.

Takeaways

1. No matter how much money you have, you will never feel that it is quite enough. (Warren Buffett is the exception.)

2. Total retirement security is unattainable because even if your income is completely certain, your future spending needs are not.

3. For a given level of savings, the safe income target is not that much less than the income target under a best-estimate scenario. This is a sign that the decumulation strategy is working.

15

ENHANCEMENT 4
A DYNAMIC SPENDING APPROACH

You might think it is always better to choose the safe income target. After all, this is your retirement we are talking about and surely it is wiser to choose the lower number and be certain (or at least 99 percent certain) of avoiding trouble. On the other hand, you could be missing out on an opportunity for a better standard of living by playing it too safe.

Retirees wrestle with this dilemma all the time. It would be nice to spend more, but not if it's going to trigger unpleasant consequences down the road. Usually, retirees resolve the matter by erring on the side of safety. They will tend to pick a spending rate that is conservative, or at least one they think will be conservative.

If they really want to play it safe, retirees let their investment income pick the spending target for them; that is, by spending only the income they can generate. As mentioned earlier, this cart-before-the-horse approach is surprisingly common, even if the outcome is not very good.

It can actually make a lot of sense to draw more income than the safe income target that was defined in Chapter 14. To do so, you need to be ready to adjust your income in case something goes wrong. The first step is to gain a better idea of the possible long-term consequences of spending a little more or a little less.

Spending Optimistically with Miserable Returns

Let's consider Carl and Hanna once again. Based on Table 14.1, their safe income target is $59,000 a year, but what if they draw income of $65,000 instead, which is a shade less than their best-estimate target? If their investment returns and lifespans prove to be middle-of-the-road rather than terrible, the $65,000 of annual income (plus inflationary adjustments) should be sustainable for life.

If their luck isn't so good, however, their savings can eventually run out. About the worst combination of circumstances involves Carl dying around age 75 and investment returns tracking the worst-case scenario that we have been using in past chapters. The outcome in this case is shown in Figure 15.1.

Figure 15.1: Where Is Carl When You Need Him?

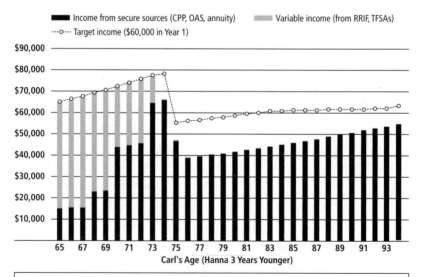

Carl and Hanna spend based on achieving a median investment return (about 5%/yr) but experience very poor returns instead. The RRIF and TFSA assets are exhausted by the time Hanna is 70. Carl dies at 75.

The chart shows that Hanna's annual income drops after Carl's death. The RRIF and TFSA assets are totally exhausted by the time Hanna is 70. At that point, all she has left is her CPP and OAS pensions plus the income from the annuity that she and Carl purchased eight years earlier. By the time she is 76, Hanna's income is about $17,000 below her target. To be clear, Carl and Hanna did not pre-emptively reduce their spending in this situation—they simply kept spending at the same rate until they ran out of RRIF and TFSA assets.

The only good news is that the gap between Hanna's income target in her later years and her actual income is smaller than it would have been, thanks to the annuity they purchased and their decision to start CPP at 70. Still, the situation is suboptimal. If Hanna encounters a rainy day event after age 70, she will have virtually no financial capacity to cope with it.

What Carl and Hanna should have done is rein in their spending in their 60s, as soon as it became clear that their investments were not performing well.

Spending Pessimistically with Good Returns

The above example would seem to imply it is better to be conservative. Before you come to that conclusion, let us look at a second example.

What if Carl and Hanna drew income at a more cautious rate such as $58,000 a year (a little less than their safe target)? This time, though, I will assume the future turns out to be more benign. Their RRIF investments achieve a median return (which is about 5 percent a year) and Carl dies at age 86 instead of 75; Hanna dies at age 91 (eight years later). The result is shown in Figure 15.2.

It would seem that spending conservatively worked out rather well for Carl and Hanna, especially Hanna. By drawing less income, they can maintain that income level throughout their retirement. In fact, Hanna has to draw more income than her income target after Carl's death because of the RRIF minimum withdrawal rules.

Figure 15.2: What if They Spend Less and Investment Returns Are Good?

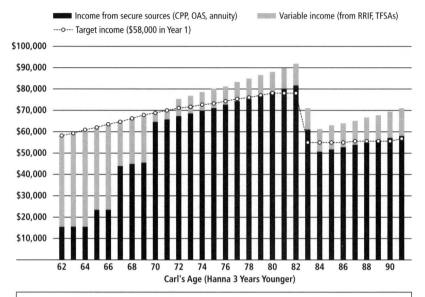

Carl and Hanna are spending based on achieving a worst-case investment return, but they achieve median returns instead. Carl dies at 86. When Hanna dies at 91, she still has over $300,000 in her RRIF and TFSA.

That's the good news. What Figure 15.2 does not show is that a sizeable surplus is building up because they are now being too conservative. At the time of death, Hanna still has more than $300,000 left in her RRIF and TFSA when she dies! Had she lived longer, the pile of unspent savings would have grown even higher. Choosing a low initial target income created a new problem for Carl and Hanna: an embarrassment of riches that materializes only when it is too late to enjoy it.

What's interesting about these two scenarios is that a fairly small change in the income they were drawing, combined with a fairly modest change in their investment results, can result in such a dramatic change in the amount of money they have left in their later years.

Describing Enhancement 4

While the two examples above seem to be exact opposites, they share a common problem: in neither case does the couple modify their drawdown rate to reflect their evolving financial situation. When their finances were deteriorating, as in the first example, Carl and Hanna should have been reducing the income they drew from their RRIF. When the financial picture was turning out fairly positive, as in the second example, they should have been increasing the amount they were drawing.

Building a massive surplus is better than running out of money, but neither outcome is ideal. Carl and Hanna should be thinking of spending a little less when economic conditions are bad and a little more when conditions are good.

The idea of actively adjusting your spending to reflect your circumstances is essential to a successful decumulation strategy. I will call this **dynamic spending**, which differs from the **static spending** that we have implicitly assumed in all the other examples I have shown so far. The idea behind dynamic spending is that a voluntary, controlled reduction in spending made early enough might enable you to avert a more drastic and involuntary cut later on. By the same token, you can increase spending if conditions warrant.

Dynamic spending means adjusting your spending rate to reflect your evolving financial situation; you would spend more if your situation is improving and less if it is deteriorating. **Static spending** involves keeping your spending rate the same, no matter what the evolving financial situation looks like.

Implementing Enhancement 4

As I mentioned in the last chapter, I had the IT team at Morneau Shepell take my Excel spreadsheets and use them to develop a sophisticated online calculation tool. This will enable anyone who is at the point of retirement (or who has retired) to calculate their personal income range. This tool is described in Appendix C and is available online at no cost at **enhancement4.morneaushepell.com.**

Dynamically adjusting your income level requires you to use the tool on a regular basis, as your safe and best estimate targets will keep on changing throughout your retirement. If you do so and stay within your income range at all times, it doesn't really matter whether your starting income is at the top end of the range (the so-called best-estimate target) or at the bottom end (the safe target) or somewhere in the middle. What matters is that you know your income range at any given age and stay within the range.

Using Enhancement 4, your income will likely drift away from your original income target over time, but that is what it should do. It will be higher than the target if things are going well, and it may be lower if things are not going so well. In the latter case, your income will still be higher in the long run than it would have been if your spending was static.

Let's apply dynamic spending to the last scenario. Starting in Year 1 of retirement, Carl and Hanna decide to draw income of $58,000 a year (plus inflationary adjustments) but actually experience median returns on their investments. Table 15.1 shows where they stand three years later when Carl is 68 and Hanna is 65 (the start of year 4). Total income has gone up to $61,900 because of inflationary adjustments.

Table 15.1: The Situation at the Start of Year 4

Savings left in the RRIF	$200,300
TFSA account balance	$64,850
Total income	$61,900

Carl and Hanna used the calculator again to re-compute their safe income target as well as their best-estimate target. Table 15.2 shows the result as of the start of Year 4.

Because of inflation, the income targets from Year 1 would have risen by Year 4 in any event. Nevertheless, the safe income target of $65,300 at the start of Year 4 is higher than what inflation alone would have produced. One reason for this is that Carl and Hanna had been playing it safe for three years by drawing income based on the $58,000 target, which was less than even their safe target. The other reason is that the returns between Year 1 and Year 4 came in at the median, which is better than what the safe target in Year 1 had assumed.

Table 15.2 How the Targets Change Over 3 Years

	Start of Year 1	Start of Year 4
Safe income target	$59,000	$65,300
Best-estimate target	$67,000	$70,800

Given the new higher targets, Carl and Hanna up their income from $55,000 a year to $65,300. They maintain this higher level of income for three more years, during which time they continue to earn investment returns at the median. They then run their numbers through the calculator once more. Their new safe target at the start of Year 7 is $72,000. Once again, this increase reflects more than inflation. It also reflects three more years of pretty good returns.

The above shows Enhancement 4 in action. Each time Carl and Hanna ran the calculator, they found they could safely spend more and started to do so. In a real-life situation, retirees might want to run the calculator more frequently, perhaps once a year. Also, they would want to keep on running it until at least age 75, at which time they might buy another annuity with half of their remaining savings, for the reasons given in Chapter 12. After another annuity purchase, most of their income is going to be secure anyway.

Analysis

Enhancement 4 is undoubtedly the most important of the four enhancements that have been described so far. Without it, your retirement income could fall to unacceptably low levels if you run into a spate of bad luck. Or you could end up with an extraordinary amount of unused (some would say wasted) capital following a sustained period of favourable conditions. Enhancement 4 makes a bad situation more tolerable and lets you capitalize on your good fortune if investments do well.

While I have indicated that the starting income can be at either the top or the bottom end of the range, I would be inclined to pick the mid-point of the range, halfway between the safe target and the best-estimate target. That may be the best way to minimize future swings in the income targets. Keep in mind that your income in retirement does not equate with your spending rate. You will have to pay income tax on at least some of that income, and while the tax bill might be modest if you have a five-figure income, it still means spending a little less than the income you draw from your savings. As previously mentioned, you will be able to calculate your personal income range at **enhancement4.morneaushepell.com**. This tool will give you an idea of how much you can actually spend rather than just how much income you can draw.

Takeaways

1. Under a static-spending approach, your spending rate (as a percentage of your income target) stays more or less the same every year. This is suboptimal because there is a good chance your assets will either run out or grow into a sizeable surplus that never gets used.

2. You always want to know your safe income target and your best-estimate target because the income you draw should always be between these two targets. Those targets will change with age.

3. The first three enhancements are important, but Enhancement 4—dynamic spending—is arguably the most important of all. It will allow you to spend more if your financial situation improves, and if the situation worsens, you will have more in reserve.

4. The amount of income you draw will usually be more than the amount you can actually spend; the difference is the income tax you have to pay.

5. The Morneau Shepell income calculation tool is a handy way to determine how much of your savings you can safely spend in a year.

16

ENHANCEMENT 5
THE NUCLEAR OPTION

The purpose of the first three enhancements is to reduce risk and increase retirement income, at least in worst-case scenarios. Enhancement 4 helps you to keep your spending on track no matter what happens.

If you do adopt all four enhancements, you will probably avoid financial catastrophe during your lifetime. But let's face it: not everyone is going to defer their CPP pension to age 70, nor will everyone buy an annuity. And maybe you need the regular services of a financial advisor, which means that your investment-related fees will be higher than if you managed an ETF portfolio on your own. On top of all this, you might fall victim to a rogue advisor who absconds with some of your life savings or, more tragically, you suffer the tragedy of the early death of your spouse. Under conditions such as these, your income in your middle retirement years might be lower than you ever contemplated. If this happens, the enhancements that have been described thus far will be rather ineffective. So now what do you do?

Desperate times call for desperate measures. The first four enhancements might be characterized as "organic," meaning that they
are geared to help you make the most of the assets you have that were
intended to produce retirement income. If organic sources of income
fall short, however, you need to tap another source.

The time may come when you need to consider using your non-
financial assets to generate income. The most common way to do
this is to take out a reverse mortgage on your home. (Assuming you
don't have any Picassos lying around that you could sell instead.)
But I can almost guarantee you won't like to do this, maybe because
it doesn't feel "organic." In spite of a number of daytime TV com-
mercials in which celebrities like Tom Selleck and Kurt Browning
tout the virtues of a reverse mortgage, it is hard to find a Canadian
who likes this option. I would be the first to agree that borrowing
against your home is not something you should do lightly; nevertheless, there will be certain situations when Enhancement 5 should
be considered.

Carl and Hanna Face an Income Gap

Let's revisit the example that was first described in Chapter 9. As
we saw in Figure 9.1, Carl and Hanna exhausted their life savings
by the time Carl was 79. After that, their annual income was a good
$30,000 a year short of their income target. For our purposes here, I
will change the circumstances a little so their situation is not quite
so dire.

First, let's assume they found a way to reduce their investment
fees from 1.80 percent down to 1.0 percent. Let's also assume they
bought an annuity with 30 percent of their RRIF assets at the point of
retirement. Finally, let's say they didn't give Arnie the $12,000 "loan"
when Carl was 73. With all these changes, their money still runs out
when Carl is 81 and Hanna is 78. The difference now is that their
annual income in future years is $24,000 shy of their target instead of
$30,000. The situation is illustrated in Figure 16.1.

Figure 16.1: Carl and Hanna Face a Big Income Gap

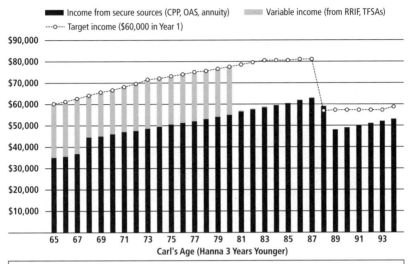

This is like Figure 9.1 except they reduced investment fees to 1% and bought an annuity. Also, they have one less spending shock. Still, the RRIF and TFSA assets run out when Carl is 80.

Let's consider Carl and Hanna's options under these straitened circumstances:

- They could resign themselves to accepting a drastic cut in spending lasting the rest of their lives.

- They could downsize and move into a smaller home, perhaps in a less expensive community. The difference in price could be used to buy an annuity to boost their income.

- They could take out a reverse mortgage.

Cutting spending by about 30 percent doesn't sound too appealing, but believe it or not, it is the path of least resistance for many people. Therefore, we cannot rule it out for Carl and Hanna. Downsizing their principal residence is a more viable option, but that becomes hard to do now that the couple is heading into their 80s. No one I know past

age 75 has any intention of moving again, except maybe to a retirement home, and that won't happen until their late 80s in most cases.

Even if they do downsize, they may not be freeing up as much
cash as they had hoped, given the myriad costs involved in selling
and moving. These costs include real estate commissions, legal fees,
some repairs and renovation costs to get the old house ready for sale
and the new place ready for moving in, moving costs, sales taxes and,
in most provinces, a land transfer tax.

Let's assume that Carl and Hanna are not prepared to slash their
budget and leave the middle class behind, nor are they willing to
downsize. That leaves them with the option of a reverse mortgage.

Reverse Mortgages Explained

If annuities are the nerds of the retirement planning world, then
reverse mortgages would be the black sheep; sort of like that distant
cousin who started smoking at 13 and writing graffiti in the school
washroom whom your mother warned you to stay away from. A
reverse mortgage is perceived negatively because it amounts to a
frontal assault on the equity in one's home, an act that is regarded
as sacrilegious in this country. We will delve into this widespread
perception a little further shortly, but first we'll start with some
basic facts.

A reverse mortgage is like a regular mortgage to the extent that
you secure a loan from a bank against the equity in your home. There
are some important differences, though. With a reverse mortgage,
you do not have to make any payments as long as you or your spouse
is still living in the house. You cannot be forced to move out. You do
have to maintain the house, however, including paying property taxes and home insurance premiums on a regular basis.

Another significant difference is in the level of interest rates. With
a regular mortgage, the five-year term fixed rate is 2.89 percent at
the time of writing (even though the posted rate is 4.64 percent). The

comparable rate for a reverse mortgage (that provides monthly payments) is 4.99 percent. The difference reflects the added risk being assumed by the bank, including the fact that they might very well not see any money coming back to them for decades. The lack of competition in the reverse mortgage market in Canada might be another reason for the big gap in interest rates as there is only one provider of this product in Canada at this time.

A third difference is the form of payment. With a regular mortgage, the bank gives you the money in a lump sum. The money from a reverse mortgage can also be received in a lump sum, although you can and should opt for a stream of regular monthly payments instead (the minimum is $500 a month). Either way, the proceeds are tax-free. We will assume Hanna chooses the monthly payments, considering that she is using the money to supplement her income.

You have to be 55 or older to qualify for a reverse mortgage and you can keep receiving income payments until the total amount owing reaches 55 percent of the equity in your home. The calculation is based on the equity in the home at the time the mortgage application is made, but the amount could be increased later if an appraisal shows the home has appreciated in value. Also, there are some set-up fees, including legal costs, which might add up to $2,500.

The bank that gives you the money will be first in line to get repaid with interest when you and your spouse have both died or if you move out. No matter how much interest has accumulated, your estate will never have to repay more than the equity in the house.

An Example

In Figure 16.1, a $24,000 a year shortfall in income first materializes when Carl is 81 and Hanna is 78. This is unlikely to come as a complete surprise to Carl and Hanna, as they would have been aware for some time that their RRIF assets were running out, so let's assume that they applied for a reverse mortgage when Carl was 78.

Figure 16.2: A Reverse Mortgage Saves the Day

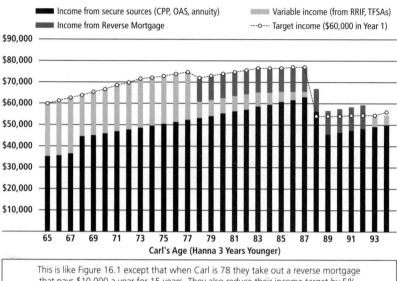

This is like Figure 16.1 except that when Carl is 78 they take out a reverse mortgage that pays $10,000 a year for 15 years. They also reduce their income target by 5%.

They take the income option and elect to receive payments of $833 a month, which is $10,000 a year and essentially tax-free. Based on the equity in their home (which is worth $500,000), they have no trouble securing monthly payments to cover the next 15 years. At the same time, they permanently reduce their income target by a modest 5 percent. As a result of these actions, the entire income shortfall is eliminated right up until Hanna is at least 91.* This is shown in Figure 16.2.

Of course, this comes at a price. The outstanding balance on the reverse mortgage grows to $222,000 by the time Hanna is 90, but the good news is that she doesn't have to pay it off while she is alive unless she decides to sell the house. If she does sell, the amount owing is easily covered by the equity in her home and there would still be about $450,000 in home equity remaining. (This assumes a 4.99-percent interest rate on the mortgage and a 2.2-percent

---

* We are assuming here that Carl died at age 88, the same as before.

annual appreciation on the home.) In fact, Hanna could probably get more income with another reverse mortgage at age 90 or later if she needed it.

Pitfalls

Perhaps reverse mortgages are now starting to look a little more respectable than that reprobate cousin. The benefits are reasonably straightforward, but let's delve a little deeper into the possible pitfalls.

First, house prices might fall or at least flatten out. If that happens, there is an outside chance the amount owing will exceed the equity in the home by the time Hanna dies or decides to sell. To minimize this risk, it is best not to start a reverse mortgage too early.

Second, the buying of a reverse mortgage is most appropriate for a homeowner who has no intention of moving again. A move would trigger a repayment with interest, and the total amount paid would be substantially greater than if a regular mortgage had been taken out instead. This is another reason not to start a reverse mortgage too early.

Third, the interest rate for the reverse mortgage might rise over time. The homeowner has little recourse but to accept the higher rates. There are no loan payments to make but the equity in the home gets drawn down just that much quicker.

Finally, the extra income from a reverse mortgage represents a potential moral hazard. It might tempt some people to indulge in a lifestyle that they may not be able to afford in the long run.

While the risks are real, the potential problems can be minimized by not taking out a reverse mortgage too early in retirement. Even though you can apply as early as 55, I suggest waiting until 75. You face some risk, however, if you wait too long. We have to acknowledge the grim reality that our financial acumen declines with age, even if the confidence we have in our cognitive abilities remains intact. If it were me (and it may be someday), I wouldn't put it off beyond age 80.

A HELOC

A home equity line of credit (HELOC) is the only other financing option that we haven't yet examined. Because a HELOC involves lower interest rates, it looks more attractive than a reverse mortgage on the surface. Whether it is viable is a different question.

With a HELOC, you take out only the money you need and the interest rate is set at the prime rate plus 0.5 percent. At the present time, the interest rate would be 3.2 percent. The trouble is that HELOCs are geared to people who have enough income to meet the regular interest payments each month. Given that insufficient retirement income is the reason Hanna is considering this option in the first place, this may be a difficult hurdle to overcome.

If the retired homeowner misses an interest payment or if the spouse dies (which reduces income from government pension sources), the bank might call in the loan. This poses just one more hurdle in using a HELOC in lieu of a reverse mortgage.

Clearly, a HELOC is not intended to be a product to help supplement the income of a cash-strapped senior. But let's say that Hanna applies for one and manages to persuade the bank to approve it. Consistent with the earlier example, the application is made when Hanna is 75, and after it is approved Hanna withdraws $850 a month to supplement her retirement income. (The $850 initial payment was chosen to ensure an apples-to-apples comparison with the reverse mortgage.) In each subsequent year, she increases her withdrawal by 3.2 percent a year. The increases are necessary because the interest payments are growing each year so the amount borrowed has to cover the increase in payments. This is shown in Table 16.1.

By the time Hanna is 90, the total amount that she has to repay is $195,000. Under the reverse mortgage, she would have had to repay $222,000. As far as retirement security is concerned, Hanna's income situation is virtually the same whether she goes with the HELOC or the reverse mortgage.

Table 16.1: Interest Payments for the HELOC

Hanna's Age	Amount Borrowed in that Year	Interest Repaid in that Year	Net Income* for Hanna in that Year
75	$10,200	$163	$10,037
76	$10,526	$495	$10,032
Etc.	Etc.	Etc.	Etc.
79	$11,570	$1,555	$10,015
84	$13,543	$3,560	$9,983
89	$15,853	$5,907	$9,946

*From the HELOC

It would, therefore, seem that by age 90, Hanna is $27,000 ahead by choosing a HELOC over a reverse mortgage. In reality, this gain is illusory. First, Hanna would probably not have been able to secure the HELOC in the first place given the low income she had after Carl died. Second, this gain is based on there being a gap of 1.79 percent between the interest rate on the reverse mortgage and the HELOC but who knows how that gap will change over time? Third, Hanna might live past 90, and if she opted for the reverse mortgage, she could stay in her home. With the HELOC, she could be forced to sell her home to pay off the outstanding loan of $195,000; that is, assuming the bank had not already called in the loan and forced her to sell years before.

The other reason why Hanna is unlikely to realize that $27,000 advantage is that the HELOC might have been too complicated to set up in the first place, especially considering the constantly increasing payments. And withdrawing more each year would be scary.

In my opinion, there is a place for both products. The HELOC makes more sense than a reverse mortgage if the borrowing is needed only for a short period. It is also preferable if the homeowner plans to move in the short to medium term. All of this, of course, pre-supposes that the HELOC can even be secured. Otherwise, you need to be thinking hard about taking out a reverse mortgage.

Takeaways

1. If all else fails, a reverse mortgage can provide much-needed income late in retirement.

2. It should only be used to provide necessary income, not to enhance one's lifestyle.

3. It is better not to secure a reverse mortgage until age 75 or so. Before that, there is still too much chance of moving again, in which case a reverse mortgage might not have been the best way to get extra income.

4. Reverse mortgages involve higher interest rates than a HELOC. At present, the gap between a reverse mortgage and a HELOC is about 180 basis points.

5. A retiree who needs income would have a hard time getting approved for a HELOC and there is always a chance that the loan may be called by the bank at an inconvenient time. It may not be a good substitute for a reverse mortgage in spite of lower interest rates.

17

A RECAP OF THE FIVE ENHANCEMENTS

Carl and Hanna have come a long way since they started on the path to a better decumulation strategy. The "Before" picture, as given in Chapter 9, was dismal.* Under a worst-case investment scenario, Carl and Hanna discovered to their dismay just how easy it was to burn through a half a million dollars of RRIF assets and another $50,000 in their TFSA account. The money was totally gone by the time Carl was 80 and Hanna was 77. They would have been about $30,000 short of their income target for the rest of their lives, and that's without indulging in any extravagant spending.

It would be easy to conclude that they didn't retire with enough money or that they should have invested more cautiously. Neither of these assertions proved to be true. As the foregoing chapters showed, all they needed was a better decumulation strategy.

With Enhancement 1 (lower fees), Carl and Hanna gave less money to investment managers and kept more of it for themselves. Enhancement 2 (CPP deferral) transferred much of the investment and longevity risk back to the government. As for the residual risk,

---

* By the way, we assumed that Carl would live until age 88 and Hanna until 95 in both the "Before" and the "After" shots.

Enhancement 3 (annuity purchase) transferred a significant portion of it to insurance companies.

It is hard to overstate the importance of these actions. To get the same level of income protection without the enhancements, Carl and Hanna would have needed about $300,000 more in assets at the point of retirement. Over the 17 years from Hanna's age 78 until her death (which we assumed would happen at 95), the couple was able to generate additional income averaging $20,000 a year by adopting the three enhancements. The result is shown in Figure 17.1.

Figure 17.1: Net Effect of Enhancements 1 to 3

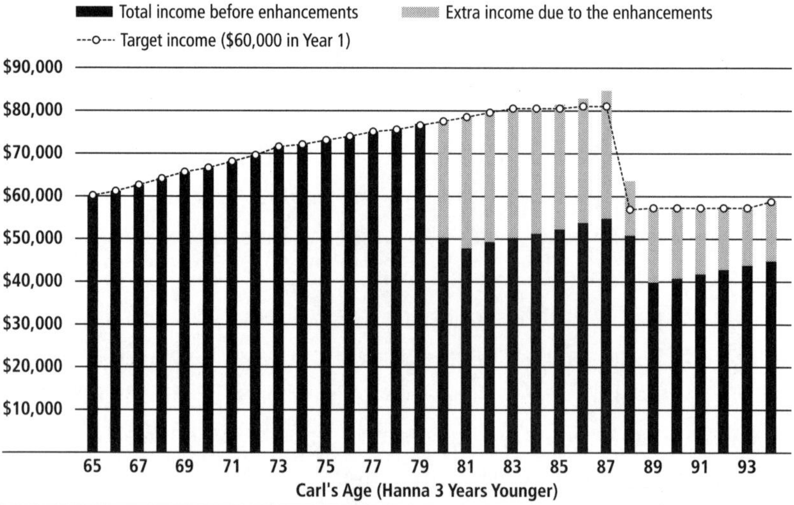

By adopting the first three enhancements, Carl and Hanna can still achieve their income target, even if a worst-case investment scenario unfolds.

The result under the worst-case scenario should be reason enough to adopt the enhancements. After all, the purpose of the enhancements was to protect against bad outcomes, not good ones. Still, it is natural to wonder what would have happened if investment returns had been better. If the investments had produced a median return in all years, would the enhancements still have helped?*

---

* Under the median scenario, the average annual return is about 5%.

First, let me point out that if investment results are at the median, Carl and Hanna reach their income target whether they adopted the enhancements or not. The enhancements still improve the situation somewhat. For the last 15 years of Hanna's life, her income would be higher by at least a few thousand dollars a year. (This is shown in Figure 17.2.) On top of that, she would have over a quarter million dollars in savings left over.

Figure 17.2: The Enhancements Help Even with Median Returns

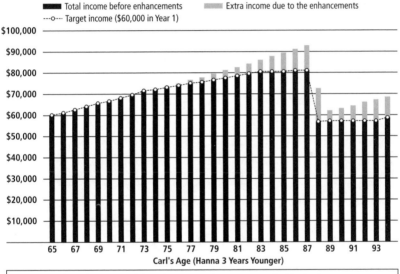

The main purpose of the enhancements is to protect against bad outcomes. But even if investment returns are fairly good, Carl and Hanna are still better off.

Some of this excess income is the result of reduced fees, but Enhancements 2 and 3 still account for more than half of it. I have to admit, I was not expecting this result. One would think that Enhancements 2 and 3 would act as a net drag on retirement income when investment results are good. After all, if you buy insurance and the insurance is not needed, then you should be worse off by an amount equal to the cost of the insurance. But this didn't happen.

Of course, there are some situations in which one is better off without Enhancements 2 and 3. This is true if long-term investment returns are well above average. But so what? With great returns, you would be doing very well with or without the enhancements. You can afford to give up a little upside potential in order to protect yourself against the downside risk.

We shouldn't ignore the other enhancements either. You need Enhancement 4 (dynamic spending) because there could be times when your financial situation will be much worse or much better than you expected. When it is worse, Enhancement 4 requires you to cut spending early so that you don't have to cut it so much later on; and if it is better, it allows you to spend more. In the real world, this could be the most important of the five enhancements that were introduced.

As for Enhancement 5—a reverse mortgage—this is a last resort, but it's one that you should be prepared to consider if the situation is dire. Even a smart decumulation strategy can fail to deliver if you don't start out with enough assets or if you experience more spending shocks than you anticipated. It is nice to know that you can still maintain your spending rate under the worst of circumstances.

As a package, the five enhancements allow the middle-income household to achieve a highly predictable income stream, no matter what the future holds. This result should go a long way toward relieving the anxiety that retirees face if they have to rely heavily on their own savings for their retirement security.

The Framing Effect

If you put yourself in the shoes of Carl and Hanna, you know you should be feeling much better about your retirement prospects after seeing the effect of the enhancements, but that probably isn't the case. You may feel that some of the enhancements go against the grain—especially CPP deferral and purchasing an annuity. As a result, you might be inclined to look for a reason to reject them. This could be true even if you concede the points I made in the foregoing chapters, when I tried to neutralize the many objections.

If this is where you're coming from, the framing effect may have something to do with it. We all have preconceived notions of right and wrong. These notions are often useful in our lives, but sometimes they get in the way of acting in our best interests. When it comes to decumulation, we should always make decisions that produce the best outcome, but this is often not what happens. The way a question or a problem is framed can dramatically affect how we respond to it.

Consider a classic experiment by the aforementioned psychologists Daniel Kahneman and Amos Tversky, both giants in the field of behavioural science. In the experiment, test subjects were told that six hundred people have a disease for which there are two possible treatments: Treatment A and Treatment B. The subjects were divided into two groups and each group was given a different explanation of the treatments.

The subjects in Group 1 were told that Treatment A would save two hundred lives. As for Treatment B, there was a 33 1/3-percent chance that everyone would be saved and a 66 2/3-percent chance that no one would be saved. Based on this explanation, 72 percent of the subjects in Group 1 chose Treatment A.

In the case of the subjects in Group 2, it was explained that four hundred patients would die under Treatment A, while Treatment B offered a 33 1/3-percent chance that no one would die and a 66 2/3-percent chance that everyone would die.

Take a minute to wrap your mind around this question. You will see that the explanations are presenting precisely the same facts; they differ only in the choice of words. In theory, Group 1 and Group 2 subjects should respond the same way, whether they heard the first explanation or the second, but that isn't what happened. In Group 2, *only 22 percent* of the subjects chose Treatment A!

How a question is asked can fundamentally change our decision, even though the basic underlying facts that are presented to us are the same. The framing effect has some major implications for retirement planning. Over time, we develop strong feelings about certain concepts, institutions or products. Some we perceive as intrinsically good and others as equally bad. If your financial advisor asked if you want to buy an annuity or defer CPP without explaining the impact in detail, your answer would almost certainly be no. Alternatively, if she asks if you are prepared to make use of all the available tools to achieve your financial goals, your answer might be different.

Corroboration

If the decumulation strategy presented in this book is so effective, you might be wondering why you don't hear much about it in the articles you read or from the financial advisors you know. That could be because the many academics and other leading pension thinkers who endorse these ideas do not tend to communicate with the general public.

The Stanford Center on Longevity, in collaboration with the Society of Actuaries, recently prepared a guide to implementing defined contribution (DC) retirement programs aimed at plan sponsors.[1] This was an American paper but the basic principles apply equally in Canada. The guide points out the value of deferring government-provided pensions and the role of annuities, two of the basic enhancements.

The Canadian Institute of Actuaries and its representatives have long recognized the importance of keeping fees low when saving for retirement (Enhancement 1). The Association of Canadian Pension Management (ACPM) has taken a leadership role in decumulation. In its recently released paper, the ACPM addresses the issues of high investment fees in retail products, the purchase of annuities and delaying CPP benefits until age 70 or older.[2] Finally, there are a number of Canadian academic papers that deal with all of the above issues.

The trouble is that these professional bodies and academics don't seem to be connecting with retirees and so the message has not filtered down to the general public. This book is an attempt to change that.

Takeaways

1. Taken together, the enhancements can significantly reduce the amount of savings one needs for retirement. Investment and longevity risk can be reduced at the same time.

2. We already know that Enhancements 2 and 3 (deferring CPP and buying an annuity) should help in a worst-case scenario because both are a form of insurance. It's a bonus that they add value even if the insurance is not needed; that is, when investment results are good.

3. The effectiveness of Enhancement 4—regulating your spending to fit your means—is harder to depict in a chart, but it could be the most important of all the enhancements.

4. Enhancement 5—converting non-financial assets to cash—is often regarded as a last resort, but you should be prepared to consider it under extreme conditions.

5. Everyone is susceptible to the framing effect, the phenomenon by which we make decisions based on how the question is asked rather than on outcomes. It can prevent us from doing what is in our best interests.

6. None of the enhancements is new, as they have been endorsed by many academics, actuaries and pension industry groups. The time has come to make them commonly accepted practice.

PART III

MAKING IT HAPPEN

18

A MESSAGE FOR EMPLOYERS

If you are an employer who sponsors a defined contribution pension plan for your employees, you should give yourself a pat on the back. You have ensured that your employees are among the "haves" in a land that is populated with "have-nots." Barely 20 percent of employees in the private sector are covered by a pension plan of any description. (A mandatory group RRSP with a significant employer contribution is almost as good.)

Never mind the constant barrage of criticism from labour groups and academics that the pension coverage offered by DC plans is inadequate, that not enough is being contributed and that employees are subject to too much risk. This is the 21st century. Individuals need to take some responsibility for their own welfare. What you are offering your employees is important as it puts them on the road toward achieving retirement income security.

The Next Step

In your role as plan sponsor, you provided significant support during the accumulation phase. You made regular contributions to the pension plan, offered a variety of investment options at an attractive cost and provided ongoing education to plan participants. With the emerging role of auto-enrolment and improved default options, employees don't even need to understand investment basics or retirement planning to accumulate an impressive account balance by retirement.

This is commendable, but why stop there? At the present time, employer support is concentrated on the accumulation phase. That support tends to end at the point of retirement when retirees are forced to find a service-provider and move their monies out of the plan into a LIF (few retirees buy an annuity). The transfer-out happens without any sponsor evaluation of the suitability of the options made available or the fees charged by the next service-provider. The employee is given no communication or decision tools to guide her. What she is given is a deadline by which her monies must be moved out.

The accumulation phase is certainly important, but as we have learned over the past 17 chapters, the decumulation phase is just as crucial and a lot more challenging. Consider the words of William Sharpe, Professor of Finance, Emeritus, at Stanford University, who is one of the originators of the capital asset pricing model, the creator of the Sharpe ratio for the analysis of risk-adjusted investment performance and the 1990 winner of the Nobel Prize in Economics. In a speech at the 2014 CFA Institute Annual Conference, Professor Sharpe said, "[Retirement income planning] is a really hard problem. It's the hardest problem I've ever looked at." If Nobel Prize winners have trouble with retirement planning, how can you leave your employees to pursue it unaided?

It is the rare individual who can navigate the dangerous waters of decumulation on his own. And in far too many cases, that individual may not be much better off in the hands of a financial advisor or mutual fund salesperson whose interests are not aligned with those of the retiree.

The Business Case for Pension Plans

Employers should remember why they established a pension plan in the first place. In part, it was done to attract and retain employees, but these have become secondary reasons. In a defined contribution world, the value of a pension plan as a retention tool has almost been neutralized, while its ability to attract talent has always been overrated relative to salary, non-pension benefits and prospects for advancement.

So why would an employer sponsor a pension plan? The real reason is that they want to see their employees do well after retirement. This is not purely an altruistic sentiment, though that is part of it; it is also good business.

Imagine having an employee who has worked diligently for your organization for thirty years. If there was no pension plan and she did not save enough on her own, she would be facing a significant drop in her standard of living. Most likely, the retiring employee would be forced to sell her home and move to a smaller place in a less attractive area. She might even resort to relying on handouts from church groups or family members to make ends meet.

If this was the typical fate of employees in your organization, your company's image in the community would take a beating. Equally important, you couldn't expect to get the best performance out of your employees who are still active. They might not have given the company pension plan much thought when they were first hired, but they are unlikely to give you their best work effort later in their careers if they feel you do not care about their welfare. So ultimately, sponsoring a pension plan is about enhancing the corporate image and improving productivity. As reasons go, these are two very good ones.

Reasons Given for Not Helping Retirees

If there is a good business case to be made for maintaining a pension plan, there should be an equally good case for ensuring that employees retire well and do not outlive their money. Yet the norm is still to focus only on the accumulation phase and to leave employees to their own devices in the decumulation phase.

Of course, there are reasons for this current practice. Employers may be leery about taking on fiduciary liability for the period after retirement; no one wants to face unnecessary litigation. In our opinion, though, the exposure is minor relative to the reward. It is also minor relative to the financial risk that is still being taken by some DB plan sponsors in terms of the volatility of their pension expense. In any event, a number of safeguards can be put in place to limit the employer's exposure in this regard as will be shown below in the "solution" section.

Another reason not to act has to do with legislative restrictions, but this is more of a historical problem. There are only two provinces that still do not allow employers to offer in-plan decumulation solutions.*

I predict that any remaining provincial restrictions (for in-plan decumulation) will soon go by the wayside and plan sponsor support in the decumulation phase will grow. No other scenario can be justified. If this book has shown anything, it is that individual employees are not going to stumble onto a smart decumulation strategy on their own while the help they get from financial advisors is inconsistent and marred by conflicts of interest.

A third reason that most employers have not yet acted is they are getting little pressure from their employees to help more. Is this surprising? There is little awareness that alternatives exist and in such a vacuum it is human nature to accept with some forbearance the circumstances in which we find ourselves. I remember when I was thirteen that it took me longer to copy work from the blackboard than my classmates. I also missed more fly balls when I was out in the schoolyard. I didn't realize it yet, but I had become quite myopic. Until I put on a pair of glasses, I had no way of knowing. Until retiring employees put on their decumulation glasses and see the possibilities, they are in the same position.

The fourth and final reason that employers have been slow to act is that the solutions have been slow to present themselves. This is changing. Effective solutions are now being created and the good

---

* The holdouts are Newfoundland & Labrador and New Brunswick. Ontario recently released draft legislation and Quebec is in the process of implementing enabling regulations.

news is that these solutions do not have to result in additional costs to the employer. Employers are using their buying power to give their employees access to institutional pricing and this is quite a gift in itself. The fees that retiring employees incur for actively managed investment funds can be slashed to less than a third of what they would be charged in the retail market.

What Should a Good Solution Look Like?

Employers are in a unique position to be able to assist their retiring employees. They have the benefit of economy of scale to provide investment options at institutional rates that are a fraction of retail fees. They can do the same with respect to making annuities available. And they can employ outside expertise at reasonable cost to offer unbiased, cutting-edge decumulation solutions, such as the ones presented in this book.

Some Canadian organizations have already shown leadership in this area and have implemented decumulation options within their retirement programs. Those options range from payment of variable pensions out of the plan to the establishment of group LIFs and group RRIFs. This is only the beginning.

Companies like Morneau Shepell are on the threshold of a next-generation response to the decumulation challenges faced by retirees. The solutions being proposed include some or all of the following elements:

- An array of passively managed, low-cost investment funds that allow the retiree to construct a diversified portfolio with his retirement savings.

- Assistance in establishing the asset mix for such a fund.

- Assistance in determining the appropriate percentage of assets to allocate for the purchase of an annuity and seeking the best price available in the insurance marketplace.

- A call centre to answer ongoing questions.

- An annual checkup that includes a review of the financial position of the retiree and whether the spending rate should be adjusted.

- Fees that are expressed as a percentage of the assets and in total are much lower than would be charged in the retail market.

Takeaways

1. Employers have an excellent business case for maintaining a pension plan for their employees. It indirectly results in better employee performance as well as a better image for the organization within the community.

2. That same business case extends naturally to the role that employers should play in support of retirees during the decumulation phase. Right now, too many employers are focused exclusively on the accumulation phase.

3. There are a variety of reasons why employers currently help so little during the decumulation phase, but the tide is turning. It should be noted that offering more support does not have to cost the employer any more.

19

Q & A ON SOME KEY POINTS

As I came to the end of writing this book, I realized some key points still had to be made. They didn't fit neatly into any of the existing chapters and, to my mind, they didn't call for a chapter of their own. I present them here as a sort of epilogue.

Q1: *It's great that things worked out so well for Carl and Hanna, but maybe this was because CPP and OAS made up such a large fraction of their overall income. What about people with more money?*

  A: I'd like to say that the decumulation strategy would be identical for people with higher income targets and more assets, but that would not be entirely true. Consider Tony and Nancy, who are distant relatives of Carl and Hanna. Tony and Nancy have combined final average earnings of $300,000 and $2.5 million in total investable assets. Their annual income target is $150,000. All of this information and more is given in Table 19.1.

Table 19.1: Data on Tony and Nancy

Nancy and Tony's age	62 and 65
Final average earnings	$300,000
Income target	$150,000
Savings in RRIFs	$1,800,000
Savings in TFSAs	$200,000
Savings that are not tax-sheltered	$500,000
CPP for Tony (% of maximum)	100%
CPP for Nancy	75%

The first thing you might notice is that their assets are more than 16 times their income target. In the case of Carl and Hanna, the multiple was a little over 9. A higher multiple is necessary as one rises up the income ladder because CPP and OAS form a smaller share of overall income.

Besides affecting the savings target disproportionately, a higher income target has several other implications. Enhancement 1, reducing fees, is even more important for high earners like Tony and Nancy because a larger share of their income will come from savings rather than from government pensions. Enhancement 2, deferring CPP until 70, is a less effective strategy, simply because the CPP pension is less important at higher income levels. It is still effective, though.

While CPP and OAS are less important to Tony and Nancy than they are to middle-income earners, the role of Enhancement 3 (annuity purchase) is just the opposite. It is more important to Tony and Nancy because their overall income is more variable. Nevertheless, I probably wouldn't recommend using more than 30 percent of one's assets to buy an annuity at retirement. It might be better to save a little cash until age 75 or so and buy some more annuity then.

Asset mix at higher income levels is also potentially more important. By this I mean that a bad outcome as a result of poor investment returns will affect Tony and Nancy more than it would Carl and Hanna. On the other hand, higher-income earners should be able to take a greater loss and still have a comfortable income. Overall, higher-income households tend to be more confident investing a greater share of their assets in stocks.

At higher income levels, the **OAS clawback** might also come into play. Its impact is marginal, however, in the case of Tony and Nancy, so we will ignore it in our projections.

OAS clawback involves the federal government taking back a portion of your OAS pensions when individual net income is over a certain threshold. In 2017, the threshold is $73,756. You would have to pay back to the government an amount equal to 15 percent of your net 2016 income over this threshold. If your net income exceeds $119,615, you have to pay back the entire amount of your OAS pension.

Another difference for high-earners is the impact of early death. In previous chapters, I showed that Hanna would be most financially vulnerable if Carl were to die in his mid-70s. That scenario is worse than if he were to die at age 90, which might have struck you as a little bizarre. After all, Hanna would have the use of all the remaining assets in the RRIF after Carl's early death. The trouble is that Carl's OAS pension is no longer payable after he dies. Also, most of his CPP pension is lost as well, except for a modest survivor benefit. The present value of these lost pension benefits exceeds half their remaining RRIF assets, which Carl would have consumed if he had lived longer.

It's different for Tony and Nancy. Their RRIF assets are much bigger, whereas the present value of the lost OAS and CPP benefits are about the same as they were for Carl and Hanna. The worst-case financial scenario (best-case human scenario) is if Tony and Nancy live past 90.

We will finish off this question with Figure 19.1. The first three enhancements greatly improve the amount of income that Tony and Nancy will receive, starting with when Nancy is 78, but this brings up another important point for higher-income couples: The chart shows the amount of income they can generate, not the amount of money they can spend. They have to pay income tax and, while the amount was almost incidental for Carl and Hanna, the tax bill can easily top 20 percent at higher income levels.

Finally, you will note in Figure 19.1 that even $2.5 million is not quite enough to meet the income target after Nancy turns 81 under a worst-case investment scenario. Not to worry, though. Tony and Nancy would have been applying Enhancement 4 throughout their retirement and would have adjusted spending downward long before an income gap developed. And besides, no gap would have materialized if their investment results were middling instead of poor.

Figure 19.1: The Enhancements Help High-Income Couples Too

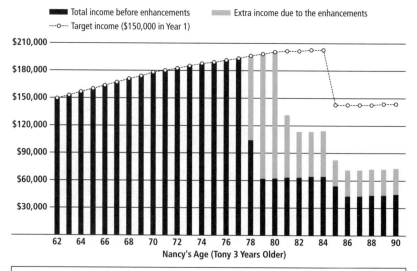

This chart shows the worst-case investment scenario, before applying Enhancement 4.

Q2: *Carl and Hanna stopped working at 65. Would deferring CPP until 70 still have been the best strategy if they continued to work past 65?*

A: For a reason that I have not been able to fathom, the Canada Pension Plan does not make it very attractive to defer CPP pension until age 70 for people who continue working. You have to keep on contributing, but you don't earn any extra pension benefits relative to someone who retires at 65 and ceases to contribute (assuming you earned the maximum CPP pension by age 65).

If you continue working past 65 but start CPP at 65, you have the choice of continuing to contribute or not, and if you do, you receive additional pension credits. This difference in treatment has the effect of neutralizing Enhancement 2 (deferring CPP past 65) or, alternatively, discouraging people from working past 65.

An example will help show just how unfair this rule is. Consider a pair of twins, Borden and Hart. Both of them worked from age 23 to age 65 and both earned enough each year to contribute the maximum to the CPP. As a result, they both qualify for the maximum CPP pension at age 65 of $1,114.17 a month (this is the maximum in effect in 2017).

Hart (who is self-employed) defers the start of his CPP pension and continues to work until 70 (in fact, he'll probably work until 85, but that's another story). As a result, he has to contribute $5,128.20 a year or more, depending on how high the CPP earnings ceiling rises. By age 70, he will have contributed at least another $25,641. The CPP pension he gets at age 70 (ignoring inflation again) is $1,582.12 a month.

Borden also defers the start of his CPP pension. The difference is that he stops working at 65. He makes no further contributions to the CPP between 65 and 70. At age 70, his CPP pension is $1,582.12 a month, the same as it is for Hart.

This is unfair to Hart. It is especially unfair because the federal government's pension plan for civil servants, the Public Service Pension Plan, doesn't allow employees to keep on contributing after 35 years of making contributions.* If the government really wants to encourage people to keep working *and* to implement an effective decumulation strategy, they had better rethink this rule.

Q3: *The examples in previous chapters were based on all retirement savings being tax-sheltered in a vehicle such as a RRIF or a LIF. What if some of the savings are after-tax monies?*

A: You will recall that the income target in the previous examples implicitly assumes that all retirement income is taxable. With retirement income of $60,000 all coming from taxable sources, expect the income tax bill for a couple to come in at 10 percent of total income, if not less. If retirement income is double that, the tax paid will be closer to 20 percent.

However, if some of the income is coming from sources where income tax has already been paid, that portion will not be taxed again. We will call such sources "after-tax assets." Examples include investments in non-registered accounts, bank accounts and assets in a TFSA.

Monies from after-tax assets go farther in retirement than monies from tax-sheltered vehicles. For instance, if your marginal tax rate in retirement is 33 percent, then an additional $1 of income from a TFSA is equivalent to $1.50 of income from a RRIF or a LIF. So if you have after-tax assets, your gross income target will be lower and so will your savings target.

It will be those from higher-income households who are most likely to have significant after-tax assets. Consider two couples, both with $2 million in assets, who are at the point

---

* Apart from a piddling 1% of salary, to help pay for the cost of total inflation protection.

of retirement. Couple A has all their assets in a RRIF, so the investment income is tax-sheltered but all withdrawals are taxable. Couple B has no tax-sheltered assets. They have $2 million in after-tax savings; assume it is in stocks.

The best estimate of sustainable retirement income for Couple A is $142,000 a year before tax (plus inflation adjustments). After tax, though, it reduces to only $114,000 a year. Couple B's investment income is taxable and so the best estimate of sustainable retirement income is $132,000 a year. Thanks to various tax credits, the after-tax amount is also $132,000 a year, so Couple B is substantially better off in spite of having less pre-tax retirement income.

Q4: *Assuming you have both tax-sheltered assets and after-tax assets, which should you use first?*

A: This is a more complicated question than it appears. The obvious answer is you should use your after-tax assets first, since the investment income on those assets is taxable. This suggests that you can maximize the growth of your total assets by preserving the tax-sheltered assets as long as possible. On the other hand, you also want to make maximum use of your tax credits because they don't carry forward. This suggests withdrawing enough of your tax-sheltered assets (which are fully taxable) to take advantage of the following tax credits: the basic personal amount, the age amount and the pension income amount. As another example, if you have enough taxable income to be flirting with the OAS clawback, you might consider deferring OAS pension until the age of 70 and drawing more of your income from your RRIF before then. You might be able to save your OAS pension from the clawback in the process. If you have significant amounts of both taxable and tax-sheltered assets, I suggest you have a discussion with your accountant about drawing them down in the most tax-efficient way.

Q5: *What if I am already 70 and have been drawing retirement income for a few years. Is it too late to make this decumulation strategy work?*

A: Clearly it is too late to put Enhancement 2 (CPP deferral) into effect if you have been receiving CPP since age 65. On the other hand, Enhancement 3 actually works better at 70 than at 65 because the mortality credit (see Chapter 12) is worth more if you buy an annuity at a later age. You took a chance by waiting until 70, but if you didn't meet up with investment disaster before that, then your inadvertent gamble paid off.

As for reducing investment fees (Enhancement 1), it is never too late to do that, but it will have less impact if you start at a later age. Enhancement 4 (dynamic spending) and Enhancement 5 (reverse mortgage) are just as relevant at 70 (or 75) as they were at 65.

Q6: *Are Carl and Hanna real people?*

A: Absolutely, though I have disguised the names and have also changed their income and assets somewhat. Nevertheless, in the writing of this book, it helped to imagine I was speaking to them directly.

Takeaways

1. Many aspects of decumulation are different at higher income levels. The savings target is a much higher multiple of the income target and deferring CPP until 70 is less effective; on the other hand, reducing investment fees, purchasing an annuity and setting the asset mix are even more important.

2. If you earn employment income past age 65, the CPP rules discourage you from deferring your CPP starting age until 70.

3. Because of income taxes, the retirement income you can produce from after-tax assets goes farther than income from tax-sheltered assets.

4. If you have significant after-tax assets, you want to draw down those assets first before touching your tax-sheltered assets.
   On the other hand, you want to take maximum advantage of your tax credits, including the basic personal amount, the age amount and the pension income amount.

20

WHERE DO YOU GO FROM HERE?

I set out with the intention of writing a book that would show readers the way to a better decumulation strategy. The enhanced retirement income strategy is now complete. The question is, how can you put it into practice? By now, you may have noticed that some of the enhancements do not lend themselves easily to a DIY approach.

For some reason, this brings to my mind a scene from *Moonstruck*, the 1987 movie starring Cher and Nicholas Cage. The scene I am thinking of takes place in the bathroom of a potential client. Mr. Castorini, the plumber (played by Vincent Gardenia), is scraping a pipe while the homeowner couple looks on anxiously. The husband finally asks, "Well, Mr. Castorini, what do you think?"

After a long pause, Castorini blurts out an astronomical cost and then explains: "There are three kinds of pipe. There's the kind you have, which is garbage, and you can see where that's gotten you. Then there's bronze, which is good, unless something goes wrong—and something *always* goes wrong. And then there's copper, which is the only pipe I use. It costs money. It costs money because it saves money."

I don't know anything about plumbing, but the most expensive option is not always the best one when it comes to investment solutions. The scene is still somewhat relevant, though, because the point is that you can go the DIY route to save money, which is good—unless something goes wrong. And maybe something doesn't always go wrong, but it can certainly happen easily enough. I would, therefore, urge caution. Financial matters are inherently more complicated than they may appear to be, and you may need a Mr. Castorini to finish the job.

The DIY Approach

Can you do it all yourself? We can break this question down between the investment function and all the other elements of the decumulation strategy. Many people invest without outside help, but a surprising number don't really know what they're doing. A high percentage of all investors think that a money market fund contains stocks (it doesn't) or that long-term bond prices go up when interest rates rise (prices go down). A whopping 75 percent cannot correctly answer the multiple choice question that starts with the words, "The benefit of owning investments that are diversified is . . . ."* Many people who purchase mutual funds are not even aware they are paying investment fees (high fees at that).

Of course, many people are quite knowledgeable about investments and you may be one of them. If so, you could choose your own basket of low-cost ETFs with an appropriate mix of stocks and bonds. As I indicated in Chapter 7, finding your way through the maze of possible fund choices online on the website of a major bank can be confusing, but it is doable.

Just be mindful that the right asset mix may depend on a number of factors. As I showed in Chapter 13, a 60-40 mix is about right if you buy an annuity with 30 percent of your assets. If you don't, the stock weighting should probably be lower than 60 percent. Second, I have assumed that interest rates will not increase much for a long time to come. If they do, the asset mix recommendation could change as

---

* The answer is: to reduce risk.

bonds would become more attractive. Finally, the optimal asset mix is not the same at all asset levels. What works for Carl and Hanna with their $500,000 in RRIF assets may not be entirely appropriate if you have $2 million.

If you think you can navigate your way through these complications, then you should be able to handle Enhancement 1.

Some of the other enhancements can also be implemented on your own, at least in principle. This is true for Enhancement 2, deferring CPP to 70. Of course, you need to have enough savings to last until age 70 to make it work and then you must have the nerve to follow through. In the five years between 65 and 70, it could be hard to watch your account balance drop month after month, which can happen when you defer the start of CPP and draw down savings instead. (Alternatively, you could continue working for a few more years, at least on a part-time basis, but not everyone wants to do that and many people don't have the opportunity to do so.) Also, you need to watch out for the rare situation when Enhancement 2 might not be advisable. In Chapter 19, I described one such situation.

Enhancement 3, buying an annuity, can also be put into action without professional help but, once again, a little guidance is useful. The type of annuity should almost certainly be of the joint and survivor form with the surviving spouse getting at least 60 percent. In some cases, the optimal percentage will be 66⅔ percent and in others it will be 100 percent. It depends in part on when the spouse dies and how much savings he or she had. It can get complicated, or you can ignore the complications and just elect a survivor benefit equal to 66⅔ percent.

The other annuity-related question is the optimal percentage of your tax-sheltered assets to allocate toward the purchase of an annuity. In my projections, I generally found that 30 percent was about right but in higher-income situations, 40 percent worked better. If you have only a moderate amount of savings, you may not have enough money to be able to implement both Enhancements 2 and 3. If it comes down to choosing between the two, I would normally recommend going with Enhancement 2.

Enhancement 5, taking out a reverse mortgage, is also simple, but you don't want to pull that trigger too early in retirement. Nor do you want to apply for more income than you need. If all goes well, you may never need Enhancement 5. I see the purpose of a reverse mortgage as a way to *maintain* your lifestyle, not to elevate it to a new level.

So, it is at least theoretically possible to implement four of the five enhancements on your own, but you have to know what you are doing and proceed with caution.

This brings us to Enhancement 4, adjusting your income to reflect your changing financial situation. As I suggested earlier, this could be the most important of all the enhancements, but you need to know your safe income target and your best-estimate target, which will change constantly for a number of reasons, not the least of which is your age.

To give the reader at least a fighting chance, Morneau Shepell has made the online tool available that will let you calculate your safe income target and your best-estimate target. If you have reached the decumulation phase, I suggest that you visit the website and try out the tool: **enhancement4.morneaushepell.com**

Alternatives to DIY

If the DIY approach makes you uncomfortable, I see three other ways in which you can proceed:

1. Go to a financial advisor with this book in hand and tell him or her that this is what you'd like to do.

2. You may be lucky enough to have an enlightened employer who believes in providing ongoing support to their retired employees.

3. The next generation of robo-advisors is very promising.

We will take a closer look at each of these options below.

Financial Advisors

In the last chapter, I indicated that many industry experts and professional associations already endorse the enhancements that are presented in this book. Unfortunately, the list does not include most financial advisors.

There are a couple of possible reasons for their general reluctance to embrace the approach outlined in Part II of this book. One is that they learned traditional strategies years ago that are less applicable today. For instance, deferring CPP until 70 is far more important today when interest rates are low than would have been the case 20 years ago.

The second reason has to do with how financial advisors are compensated. Most of them receive a fee based on a percentage of the assets invested and so, as a result, their interests are not aligned with yours during the decumulation stage. It is easy to see why they won't be thrilled with Enhancement 1 (reduced fees) or Enhancement 2 (deferring CPP, which draws down your savings more quickly). They won't even like Enhancement 3 much; the annuity purchase provides a commission, but it is a one-time event so it reduces the advisor's ongoing revenue stream. The same goes with Enhancement 5, reverse mortgages.

The only enhancement that doesn't reduce fees is Enhancement 4 (dynamic spending), but this is not financially rewarding to financial advisors either. They don't get paid any more to help you adjust your spending and it can involve a lot of extra time and effort on their part.

This state of affairs is unfortunate because financial advisors are the natural source for advice (at least until robo-advisors are up to speed). I'm not saying that all financial advisors are uncooperative. Fee-based advisors will certainly be more amenable. Even some commission-based advisors are able to look past the impact on their own remuneration and help their clients implement the strategies I have described in this book.

So you may want to give your financial advisor a try first. You might even suggest they read a copy of this book if they haven't seen it yet. If they really have your best interests at heart, they just might buy into it.

I am less optimistic about this if your advisor has put you into mutual funds that contain a **deferred sales charge (DSC)**. To me, this is one of the most odious practices a fund salesperson can perpetrate on an innocent investor. DSCs saddle you with high fees and take away the freedom to move your monies from one fund family to another. Anyone who has put you into funds that have a DSC is unlikely to be a good source for unbiased decumulation advice.

A **deferred sales charge (DSC)** is a rather large commission that a mutual fund salesperson receives upfront. If you change your mind and try to move to another fund family within a certain period (about six years), you are charged a hefty redemption penalty. On $500,000 of investments, the fee could be $20,000 or more. The salesperson may say it is for your own protection—so you don't jump from one investment to another too often—but this is like a third-world employer saying that he locks in his migrant employees at night "for their own protection."

The Employer Route

It is possible that you accumulated most of your savings in an employer-sponsored group plan. This would be either a group RRSP or a defined contribution pension plan. If your employer provides ongoing support after retirement at no cost to you, you should probably take them up on it. Employers tend to have your best interests at heart and they also have access to objective expertise at reasonable cost.

The type of support available to you may include ongoing investment education and help with your decumulation strategy. You should also see if you can keep your money in the employer-sponsored retirement plan after retirement. As mentioned in Chapter 18, that route might give you the best deal in terms of investment fees.

Robo-Advisors

A robo-advisor (also known as an "automated investment advisor") is a computer program that enables you to set your asset mix and choose your funds in accordance with that mix. This is all done with little or no human supervision.

Examples of companies in the business are Wealthsimple and Questrade. To get started, you go online and answer a series of questions that help the computer program establish your financial situation, investment knowledge and risk tolerance. Then once you register for an account, you are on your way.

The main attraction of a robo-advisor is price, as the ongoing fee is about 50 basis points plus the cost of the ETFs themselves. In some cases, clients with more investable assets ($150,000 or so) pay a lower fee, such as 40 basis points. This is only marginally more expensive and a lot safer than trying to do it on your own. Moreover, you are saving 50 to 100 basis points (or more) compared to going to a traditional financial advisor. As we saw with Enhancement 1, even fee savings of that magnitude can make a big difference in your ultimate retirement income.

I can certainly understand why a lot of investors might have qualms about using a robo-advisor. We still like the human touch with any transaction because automated interfaces can be highly frustrating. In addition, Hollywood has conditioned us to think of intelligent machines as the enemy of mankind (e.g., *The Terminator*) or prone to act contrary to our best interests (e.g., HAL in *2001: A Space Odyssey*).

Even if they are not evil, we tend to think of machines as being very limited in their abilities compared with humans. But that is changing rapidly. "Machine learning" and "deep learning" are boosting the capabilities of computers beyond anything we thought possible just a few years ago. Garry Kasparov (former world chess champion) didn't think IBM's Deep Blue could beat him. Artificially intelligent lawyers, such as ROSS (built on IBM's Watson), can read and understand complicated legal documents, answer questions based on them and cite references to support the answers. Babylon's chatbot can diagnose patients more quickly and more accurately than physicians. What is even more impressive is that these AI systems get better the more they are used.

The real drawback with today's generation of robo-advisors in the financial space is that they do not handle all aspects of financial planning. The area of decumulation in particular has not yet been fully explored. The robo-advisors out there today do a reasonably good job of helping you manage assets, which is fine as far as it goes; but what we really need are better algorithms that can help with all the enhancements that were described in Part II. This includes assessing whether Enhancements 2 and 3 are right for you and then helping you to implement them. Even more important, they would ideally handle Enhancement 4—dynamic spending. The fact that robo-advisors don't deal with this today has nothing to do with limitations in the capabilities of modern computers. Compared to AI lawyers and medical diagnoses, decumulation is child's play. As the financial industry starts to turn its attention to decumulation (rather than its current focus on accumulation), better tools will be available to retirees. For now, I humbly believe Morneau Shepell's calculation tool, as described in Appendix C, is the best decumulation calculator available.

Takeaways

1. There are four ways to bring to life the decumulation strategy recommended in this book: the DIY approach, through financial advisors, through your employer or with the next generation of robo-advisors.

2. The DIY approach is cheapest, but you need to navigate around the pitfalls.

3. Financial advisors are the most natural place to look for help, but the solutions presented in this book may conflict with how

they are remunerated. The cost of an advisor also neutralizes the benefits of Enhancement 1.

4. If you accumulated most of your savings through a workplace plan, your employer may be prepared to offer ongoing support, at least to see you through the transition into retirement. You should probably use it.

5. Robo-advisors are already useful for setting asset mix and managing an investment portfolio. The next generation of robo-advisors will no doubt help with all aspects of the decumulation phase, especially the implementation of Enhancement 4.

6. Morneau Shepell's calculation tool is our attempt to help individuals implement Enhancement 4 on their own.

APPENDIX A
SUMMARY OF TAKEAWAYS

Chapter 1: Spending Is Not as Easy as It Sounds

1. Decumulation is not as straightforward as you might think; by comparison, the accumulation phase is child's play.

2. Disaster can strike even if you save a great deal, wait until 65 to retire and follow a widely accepted decumulation strategy.

3. The good news is that disaster can be averted with a better decumulation strategy (to be rolled out in the following chapters).

Chapter 2: What Type of Retiree Are You?

1. Spending in retirement falls into three categories or "buckets": regular spending, rainy day spending and bequests.

2. There are at least four types of retirees; the type of retiree you are dictates the priority you place on each spending bucket.

3. It is wise to know your retirement type before you formulate a decumulation strategy.

4. A good decumulation strategy maximizes the portion of your income that is stable and predictable. This is a sure-fire way of allaying your financial anxiety after retirement.

Chapter 3: Your Income Target in Year One

1. If you saved regularly, raised children and made mortgage payments, your retirement income target is unlikely to be as high as 70 percent of final pay, or even 60 percent.

2. You should know your own retirement income target. It helps you to calibrate your withdrawal rate after retirement. Before retirement, that knowledge should reduce your anxiety about your state of retirement-readiness.

3. You may have a few golden years before retiring when you are free of mortgage payments and child-raising costs. Before you hurry out to spend the extra cash, figure out your retirement income target and make sure you save enough to reach it.

4. The higher you set your retirement income target, the more you need to save while you're working and, therefore, the less you can spend before you retire. You need to strike a balance.

Chapter 4: Your Retirement Income Target in Future Years

1. The amount of retirement income you need tends to rise more slowly than inflation, especially between ages 70 and 90.

2. You want to determine your ideal retirement income target as well as the lowest level of income that you would be prepared to accept. You also want to know how these will change in the later stages of retirement.

3. The income that you generate from your savings does not need to be fully indexed to inflation.

4. The acceptable income zone can be a little higher or a little lower depending on the type of retiree you are.

Chapter 5: Rainy Day Spending

1. The financial shocks you are most likely to encounter in retirement tend to be small enough to be manageable.

2. The really big shocks tend to be events involving family members, like divorce or bailing out a grown-up child. The incidence of these types of shocks tends to be low or, in the case of helping children, within your control.

3. Hold back about 3 to 5 percent of your retirement income each year and keep it in a separate account to be used exclusively for rainy day spending.

Chapter 6: Planning an Inheritance

1. You pay a price for making a large bequest. It can restrict your choice of investment vehicles at retirement and reduce your retirement income.

2. You should be drawing down your financial assets as you get older, which means the bequest you can make will gradually become smaller. This works out well because your children's need for the money should also diminish as they progress into later adulthood.

3. Be clear as to how much money really needs to be passed down to your children. If you or your spouse lives a long time, a bequest may be more useful in the hands of your grandchildren.

4. Don't forget about the equity in the home. It may be locked-in while you are alive, but it can be turned into cash after you and your spouse die. This may be all the inheritance your children will ever need.

Chapter 7: Investment Risk

1. It is hard to avoid investing in stocks if you want a decent return on your savings.

2. If you have a diversified portfolio of stocks and bonds, you will probably be able to survive even a market disaster as severe as the crash of 1929.

3. Stay away from investing in second mortgages.

4. Real estate investment can be lucrative for long-term investors, but it is not for amateurs.

5. You might invest some of your savings in T-bills or other short-term investments, but only a smallish portion. The same goes with real return bonds.

6. Long-term Government of Canada bonds are unlikely to do well for many years to come, but they still tend to form part of most investment portfolios.

7. The median return on a portfolio of stocks and bonds is likely to be just 5 to 5.5 percent a year in the longer term, and this is before fees.

8. Since we seem to be mired in an environment of low interest rates and low investment returns for the long term, you cannot afford to pay a lot in investment fees.

9. Invest only in pooled funds or ETFs that represent the entire market. Do not try to pick your own stocks, even with the help of a broker.

Chapter 8: What Not to Do

1. Investment losses will happen every so often; a good decumulation strategy should be able to absorb them.

2. Withdrawing the minimum amount permitted under the RRIF rules is not a bad approach to decumulation, but the chapters to come will show you can do better.

3. Withdrawing the same percentage of assets each year does not work well. In general, you should expect to withdraw an increasing percentage with age.

4. You may be tempted to spend only the investment income and leave the principal intact, but this strategy makes sense only at the extremes of wealth. It is not recommended for those in the middle-income range.

5. You need to find a way to incorporate both your income target and your available assets into your decumulation strategy—not just one or the other.

Chapter 9: Setting the Stage

1. Money has diminishing utility the higher your income level. It is more important to avoid falling short than it is to generate excess income.

2. A good starting point for a decumulation strategy is the RRIF minimum withdrawal schedule. You just want to enhance it to better reflect your income needs.

Chapter 10: Enhancement 1—Reducing Fees

1. Investment fees can have a big impact on how much retirement income one can generate from a given amount of savings.

2. Fees for actively managed mutual funds typically range from 1.5 percent a year to more than 3 percent, depending on the fund family and whether a financial advisor is involved.

3. Tangible evidence of added value from active management is hard to find.

4. Using passively managed ETFs, the total annual investment fee can be brought down to about 50 basis points.

Chapter 11: Enhancement 2—Deferring CPP Pension

1. Enhancement 2 entails postponing the start of your CPP pension until 70.

2. By doing so, CPP income is increased by nearly 50 percent in the case of someone who contributed to CPP until age 65. This increased pension is inflation-protected and payable for life.

3. Under Enhancement 2, you are essentially transferring some of your investment risk and longevity risk back to the government and are doing so at zero cost.

4. In spite of these advantages, very few Canadians postpone their CPP until 70. There are many plausible reasons why they reject this option, but few good reasons for those who have the financial means to wait until 70 to collect their CPP.

5. You need substantial savings to be able to adopt Enhancement 2. In the case of a couple, it is roughly $200,000.

Chapter 12: Enhancement 3—Buying an Annuity

1. Unless you have a very large amount of savings, at least 60 percent of the annuity you buy should continue to be paid to the surviving spouse. This measure makes up for the loss of the deceased spouse's CPP and OAS income.

2. It is better to buy a non-indexed annuity.

3. Buying an annuity upon your retirement with about 30 percent of your RRIF assets will ensure you have more retirement income in the event that future investment returns are truly bad.

4. Survivor benefits in the event of a spouse's early death also tend to be a little better if you buy an annuity than if you do not.

5. There is an opportunity cost to buying an annuity: you will not have as big a windfall within your RRIF if investments do really well, but you will still have more income than you had expected.

6. If you don't mind taking some risk, there is a case to be made for waiting until age 75 to buy the annuity or at least for buying a second annuity then, even if you bought one at the point of retirement. The mortality credit at age 75 improves your odds of receiving more income with less risk.

Chapter 13: Fine-Tuning the Asset Mix

1. When assessing your asset mix in retirement, remember to include the value of the annuity as part of your overall portfolio and consider it equivalent to investing in bonds.

2. If you want an overall asset mix of 50-50, you may want to increase the stock weighting in the RRIF to 70 percent. To get to an overall mix of 40-60, the asset mix in the RRIF should be about 60-40.

3. Under a worst-case investment scenario, there is little difference in outcome whether the RRIF has a 50-50 asset mix or 70-30. A mix of 70-30 produces a slightly better result if you enjoy a median return and a much better result if returns are well above average.

4. As the RRIF assets get drawn down between ages 65 and 70, the stock weighting in the overall portfolio will automatically shrink. You may, therefore, not want to reduce the stock weighting in your RRIF before age 70.

Chapter 14: Did You Save Enough?

1. No matter how much money you have, you will never feel it is quite enough. Warren Buffett is the exception.

2. Total retirement security is unattainable because even if your income is completely certain, your future spending needs are not.

3. For a given level of savings, the safe income target is not that much less than the income target under a best-estimate scenario. This is a sign that the decumulation strategy is working.

Chapter 15: Enhancement 4—A Dynamic Spending Approach

1. Under a static-spending approach, your spending rate (as a percentage of your income target) stays more or less the same every year. This is suboptimal because there is a good chance your assets will either run out or grow into a sizeable surplus that never gets used.

2. You always want to know your safe income target and your best-estimate target because the income you draw should always be between these two targets. Those targets will change with age.

3. The first three enhancements are important, but Enhancement 4—dynamic spending—is arguably the most important of all. It will allow you to spend more if your financial situation improves; and if the situation worsens, you will have more in reserve.

Chapter 16: Enhancement 5—The Nuclear Option

1. If all else fails, a reverse mortgage can provide much-needed income late in retirement.

2. It should only be used to provide necessary income, not to enhance one's lifestyle.

3. It is better not to secure a reverse mortgage until age 75 or so. Before that, there is still too much chance of moving again, in which case a reverse mortgage might not have been the best way to get extra income.

4. Reverse mortgages involve higher interest rates than a HELOC. At present, the gap between a reverse mortgage and a HELOC is about 180 basis points.

5. A retiree who needs income would have a hard time getting approved for a HELOC, and there is always a chance that the loan may be called by the bank at an inconvenient time. It may not be a good substitute for a reverse mortgage in spite of lower interest rates.

Chapter 17: A Recap of the Five Enhancements

1. Taken together, the enhancements can significantly reduce the amount of savings one needs for retirement. Investment and longevity risk can be reduced at the same time.

2. We already know that Enhancements 2 and 3 (deferring CPP and buying an annuity) should help in a worst-case scenario because both are a form of insurance. It is a bonus that they add value even if the insurance is not needed; that is, when investment results are good.

3. The effectiveness of Enhancement 4—regulating your spending to fit your means—is harder to depict in a chart, but it could be the most important of all the enhancements.

4. Enhancement 5—converting non-financial assets to cash—is often regarded as a last resort, but you should be prepared to consider it under extreme conditions.

5. Everyone is susceptible to the framing effect, the phenomenon in which we make decisions based on how the question is asked rather than on outcomes. It can prevent us from doing what is in our best interests.

6. None of the enhancements is new, as they have been endorsed by many academics, actuaries and pension industry groups. The time has come to make them commonly accepted practice.

Chapter 18: A Message for Employers

1. Employers have an excellent business case for maintaining a pension plan for their employees. It indirectly results in better employee performance as well as a better image for the organization within the community.

2. That same business case extends naturally to the role employers should play in support of retirees during the decumulation phase. Right now, too many employers are focused exclusively on the accumulation phase.

3. There are a variety of reasons why employers currently help so little during the decumulation phase, but the tide is turning. It should be noted that offering more support does not have to cost the employer any more.

Chapter 19: Q & A on Some Key Points

1. Many aspects of decumulation are different at higher income levels. The savings target is a much higher multiple of the income target and deferring CPP until 70 is less effective; on the other hand, reducing investment fees, purchasing an annuity and setting the asset mix are even more important.

2. If you earn employment income past age 65, the CPP rules discourage you from deferring your CPP starting age until 70.

3. Because of income taxes, the retirement income you can produce from after-tax assets goes farther than income from tax-sheltered assets.

4. If you have significant after-tax assets, you want to draw those down first before your tax-sheltered assets. If you have enough after-tax assets to allow you to defer CPP pension until 70, you might not want to open a RRIF until as late as possible, which is at age 71.

Chapter 20: Where Do You Go From Here?

1. There are four ways to bring to life the decumulation strategy recommended in this book: the DIY approach, through financial advisors, through your employer or with the next generation of robo-advisors.

2. The DIY approach is cheapest, but you need to navigate around the pitfalls.

3. Financial advisors are the most natural place to look for help, but the solutions presented in this book may conflict with how they are remunerated. The cost of an advisor also neutralizes the benefits of Enhancement 1.

4. If you accumulated most of your savings through a workplace plan, your employer may be prepared to offer ongoing support, at least to see you through the transition into retirement. You should probably use it.

5. Robo-advisors are already useful for setting asset mix and managing an investment portfolio. The next generation of robo-advisors will no doubt help with all aspects of the decumulation phase, especially the implementation of Enhancement 4.

APPENDIX B
SUMMARY OF LIFS AND RRIFS

This Appendix summarizes the rules for the various registered retirement vehicles you might use during the decumulation phase.

Overview

The vehicle you use in the decumulation phase depends in part on where the money came from. If you were saving for retirement in an RRSP, the money will eventually be transferred to a RRIF, used to purchase a life annuity or some combination of the two. You can also transfer monies initially to a RRIF and then decide a few years later to buy an annuity with some or all of the remaining RRIF assets.

If the savings vehicle was a defined contribution (DC) pension plan, the decumulation vehicle will probably be a life income fund (LIF) or equivalent (some provinces call it something else). I say probably because you may have the option of keeping the monies in your employer's pension plan. This might be a very good thing to do because your employer's plan will probably entail lower fees. Alternatively, you can use your DC pension plan balance to buy an annuity. We will ignore the annuity option here because it was addressed in Chapter 12.

RRIF Basics

A RRIF is very much like an RRSP but operating in reverse. The basic purpose of an RRSP is to build your retirement savings. The basic purpose of a RRIF is to draw it down; you cannot contribute to a RRIF. What the two vehicles have in common is the choice of investment options and the fact that the investment income is tax-sheltered.

When you are ready to start drawing an income, you would close your RRSP account and transfer the money to a RRIF. This rollover into a RRIF occurs tax-free. You must start making minimum withdrawals from your RRIF by December 31 of the following year. The earliest you can start to receive payments from a RRIF is at age 55. Once you start, the amount you withdraw each year can be no less than a minimum percentage that depends on your age. These percentages are shown in Table B.1 and are applied to the RRIF balance at the beginning of the year. Withdrawals can be made once a year, semi-annually, quarterly or monthly.* Additional withdrawals are also permitted. You could also choose to withdraw the entire RRIF balance all in one year.

If you do not need the RRIF income, it may be best to keep the money in your RRSP. You no longer have that choice, however, when you turn 71. Your RRSP must be closed and the amount transferred to a RRIF by December 31 of the year in which you turn 71. You don't have to make a withdrawal from the RRIF until December 31 of the following calendar year. As a result, your first withdrawal from a RRIF does not have to occur until you are 72.

It is important to note that you have the option to base your minimum withdrawals on your spouse's age rather than your own age. This can be useful if your spouse is younger and you are trying to minimize your RRIF withdrawals. For example, if you were 72 on January 1, the minimum payout from your RRIF that year would normally be 5.40 percent. If your spouse was age 66, for example, your minimum payout that year could be reduced to 4.17 percent.

---

* If you like formulas, the minimum withdrawal between ages 55 and 70 is derived by taking your RRIF balance at the start of the year and dividing it by X, where X = (90 – age).

Table B.1: Minimum Annual Withdrawals from a RRIF

Age	Min. Annual Withdrawal	Age	Min. Annual Withdrawal
55	2.86%	76	5.98%
56	2.94%	77	6.17%
57	3.03%	78	6.36%
58	3.13%	79	6.58%
59	3.23%	80	6.82%
60	3.33%	81	7.08%
61	3.45%	82	7.38%
62	3.57%	83	7.71%
63	3.70%	84	8.08%
64	3.85%	85	8.51%
65	4.00%	86	8.99%
66	4.17%	87	9.55%
67	4.35%	88	10.21%
68	4.55%	89	10.99%
69	4.76%	90	11.92%
70	5.00%	91	13.06%
71	5.28%	92	14.49%
72	5.40%	93	16.34%
73	5.53%	94	18.79%
74	5.67%	95	20%
75	5.82%	Over 95	20%

RRIF Investments

A RRIF isn't an investment itself. It is an account that holds investments. A RRIF can be invested in a daily interest account, GICs, mutual funds, ETFs or individual stocks and bonds.

Taxation of a RRIF

All withdrawals from a RRIF are considered taxable income. For tax purposes, however, transfers between vehicles are not considered to be withdrawals. As a result, the one-time rollover from an RRSP to a RRIF is not taxed, nor is the use of RRIF assets to purchase an annuity.

If you draw only the minimum in a given year, you do not have to pay a withholding tax. If you withdraw more than the minimum amount, the withholding tax on the excess withdrawal is calculated based on the rates in Table B.2. Note that in the first calendar year of the RRIF, the minimum is nil, which means tax will be withheld.

Table B.2: Withholding Tax*

Excess Withdrawn	Withholding Tax
Up to $5,000	10%
$5,000 to $15,000	20%
Over $15,000	30%

*Different percentages apply in Quebec.

Withdrawals in Kind

If you are withdrawing only the minimum from your RRIF and do not need the money immediately, you can transfer it "in kind" to a TFSA or a non-registered account. This can be useful if all the money in the RRIF is fully invested and you don't want to pay redemption fees or other transaction fees by liquidating it before making the withdrawal. Your institution might still require you to pay a redemption fee and you are still required to report the in-kind transfer as taxable income.

When You Die

If you have a spouse at the time of death, your spouse can become the owner of your RRIF and would receive future payments. If you have no spouse, the RRIF must be collapsed on death and the proceeds paid to your named beneficiary or, if there is none, to your estate. The amount would be fully taxable except if the beneficiary is a financially dependent child or grandchild who is (a) under 18 or (b) dependent due to an infirmity.

Analysis of RRIF Rules

For many retirees, the knee-jerk reaction has been to pay the minimum amount of income tax from their retirement savings. This can lead to keeping the money in an RRSP until the age of 71 and then making the minimum withdrawals from the RRIF from age 72 and on. This practice, of course, has nothing to do with the strategies presented in this book. What I proposed in Chapter 11 is in fact very close to the opposite. Enhancement 2 was based on deferring CPP pension until age 70 and drawing down your RRIF instead.

Still, the idea of delaying and then minimizing RRIF payouts could still be compatible with Enhancement 2, provided that you have other sources of income to tide you over until age 70. This idea was explored in Chapter 19.

Life Income Funds (LIFs)

If your retirement savings came from a pension plan rather than an RRSP, you might transfer the account balance to a locked-in retirement account (LIRA) or a locked-in RRSP where it would remain tax-sheltered until you are ready to start receiving payouts or until age 71, if earlier. When that time comes, the monies would be transferred to a LIF or the equivalent vehicle in that jurisdiction.

A LIF serves the same purpose as a RRIF. Both are vehicles from which you can receive regular income with the savings you accumulated. One fundamental difference is that LIF withdrawals are subject to a maximum percentage of assets (except in Saskatchewan). This means that the amount you can take out in a given year may be capped. All LIFs and equivalent vehicles are subject to the same minimum annual withdrawal as RRIFs, stated as a percentage of total assets as specified in Table B.1, above.

Equivalent Vehicles

LIF rules differ from province to province because the assets come from registered pension plans, which are subject to provincial pension legislation; in the case of federally regulated organizations, the LIF rules are the responsibility of the federal government. These variations by jurisdiction can make LIFs or their equivalent seem much more complicated. The best thing to do is to locate the rules below that pertain to your situation and filter out the rest.

In Newfoundland & Labrador, retirees also have the option of transferring their money to a locked-in retirement income fund (LRIF). Saskatchewan replaced LIFs with prescribed retirement income funds (PRIFs). LIFs still exist in the case of federally regulated organizations but have been displaced by restricted life income funds (RLIFs) to some extent. LRIFs, PRIFs and RLIFs are all similar to LIFs except as indicated below.

Duration of a LIF

In Newfoundland & Labrador and Saskatchewan, remaining LIF funds at one time had to be used to purchase a life annuity at age 80. With the new vehicles (LRIFs and PRIFs respectively), this is no longer a requirement. Prince Edward Island has no LIF at all because it never enacted pension legislation. As a result, a RRIF is the only option available there. In all other provinces, a LIF normally continues for life unless the LIF holder withdraws the entire balance in cash when permissible or uses it to buy an annuity. Annuities purchased with LIFs might differ from annuities purchased with funds from RRIFs because certain spousal survivor benefits need to be included in the case of a LIF (unless the spouse waived them).

Cash-Out Options

Most jurisdictions allow LIF holders to transfer a portion of the LIF to a regular RRSP or a RRIF. If you want to pursue the decumulation strategy in this book, this option can be very important. Otherwise, the LIF maximum withdrawal rules in most jurisdictions make it difficult if not impossible to put Enhancement 2 into effect (deferring CPP).

In Ontario, the LIF holder has the one-time option of transferring up to 50 percent of the LIF assets into a regular RRSP or a RRIF. The election must be within 60 days of transferring locked-in funds from a LIRA or a registered pension plan into the LIF. Alberta also gives the option to transfer up to 50 percent of locked-in assets to an RRSP or a RRIF, provided the LIF holder does so before transferring the rest of the assets to a LIF.

Before age 65, Quebecers can withdraw an additional amount from their LIFs equal to 40 percent of the Quebec pensionable earnings ceiling in that year. This supplement tides them over until government pensions start. Unfortunately, they do not have this option between the ages of 65 and 70, when it could be helpful in carrying out Enhancement 2.

In New Brunswick, the LIF owner has the one-time option to transfer LIF assets to a RRIF. The maximum transfer is three times the maximum withdrawal in that year or 25 percent of the LIF balance at the start of the year, whichever is less.

Manitoba LIF holders can make a one-time transfer to a PRIF of up to 50 percent of the value of their LIF. There are no restrictions within the PRIF as to how much can be withdrawn in a given year. In Saskatchewan, the PRIF has replaced the LIF. That makes Saskatchewan the only province with no restrictions on the amount that can be withdrawn in a given year.

If you worked for a federally regulated employer (for example, in transportation, banking or communications), you can transfer your LIF assets to an RLIF. This is like a LIF except you have the one-time opportunity to transfer 50 percent of the assets to a regular RRSP or RRIF. This option must be elected within 60 days of opening the RLIF.

Maximum Annual Payouts

Payouts under a LIF are subject to a maximum (except in Saskatchewan). The maximum in a given year is calculated by dividing the LIF balance by an **annuity certain** factor. The term of the annuity is the number of years until the age of 90. The interest rate for the annuity is based on the CANSIM (Canadian socioeconomic database from Statistics Canada) interest rate from the preceding November or 6 percent, if greater. There are slight variations in some jurisdictions, as described below.

An **annuity certain** is a stream of payments (usually equal) that is made for a fixed period, such as 10 years. It differs from a life annuity, which is payable until death. The payments are based on a certain interest rate; the higher the rate, the higher the payments.

This is probably more information than you need to know. What is worth knowing is that the maximum withdrawal percentages will probably not change for many years to come. With interest rates so low, the 6-percent default rate underlying the annuity certain will be the applicable rate for the foreseeable future. The federal jurisdiction is the exception, as the 6-percent default rate does not apply. As a result, their maximum percentages are significantly lower (this includes PEI, which has no pension legislation of its own). Finally, the basis for the calculation is a little different in Quebec, Manitoba and Nova Scotia.

Table B.3 shows the maximum percentage of assets that can be paid out of a LIF for each year from age 55 and on. For example, someone at age 58 in Manitoba can withdraw no more than 6.6 percent of her LIF assets in that year. Note that some provinces allow LIF payments before 55, but this is not shown here.

In British Columbia, Alberta, Manitoba and Ontario, the maximum payment is the investment return in the previous year if that amount is greater than the percentage given in Table B.3. In Newfoundland & Labrador, the maximum payment on an LRIF is the investment return from the previous year. This means that the maximum will equal the minimum in most years, especially after age 70.

Table B.3: Maximum Withdrawal Percentages

Age	Quebec, Manitoba and Nova Scotia	All Other Provinces*	Age	Quebec, Manitoba and Nova Scotia	All Other Provinces*
55	6.40%	6.51%	73	8.50%	9.00%
56	6.50%	6.57%	74	8.80%	9.34%
57	6.50%	6.63%	75	9.10%	9.71%
58	6.60%	6.70%	76	9.40%	10.15%
59	6.70%	6.77%	77	9.80%	10.66%
60	6.70%	6.85%	78	10.20%	11.25%
61	6.80%	6.94%	79	10.80%	11.96%
62	6.90%	7.04%	80	11.50%	12.82%
63	7.00%	7.14%	81	12.10%	13.87%
64	7.10%	7.26%	82	12.90%	15.19%
65	7.20%	7.38%	83	13.80%	16.90%
66	7.30%	7.52%	84	14.80%	19.19%
67	7.40%	7.67%	85	16.00%	22.40%
68	7.60%	7.83%	86	17.30%	27.23%
69	7.70%	8.02%	87	18.90%	35.29%
70	7.90%	8.22%	88	20.00%	51.46%
71	8.10%	8.45%	89	20.00%	100.00%
72	8.30%	8.71%	90+	20.00%	100.00%

* Except for federal jurisdiction, Newfoundland & Labrador and the province of PEI, where the maximum is much lower. Also, the table does not reflect the modification to the maximum due to the previous year's investment return.

Analysis of LIFs

It is ironic that the maximum withdrawal rules do exactly the opposite of what they are intended to do. They are meant to enhance retirement security by ensuring that retirees don't outlive their assets. Unfortunately, the maximums make it more difficult to implement Enhancement 2, deferring CPP. Fortunately, most retirees can get around this restriction by using the LIF cash-out option that is available in most jurisdictions coupled with the use of other assets such as TFSAs, RRSPs and non-registered assets to generate income until they start CPP payments at age 70.

APPENDIX C
IMPLEMENTING ENHANCEMENT 4
WITH MORNEAU SHEPELL'S INCOME
CALCULATOR

As described in Chapter 15, Enhancement 4 involves continually adjusting your spending rate so that you always stay within your means while getting the most out of your savings. You always want to keep your income between what I call the safe income target and the best-estimate target. Throughout your retirement these two targets will change as your assets change. They may also change for other reasons, such as the death of a spouse.

This appendix will help you to understand Morneau Shepell's retirement income calculator better and will provide some guidance as to when you would use it. One of the important things the calculator does is estimate the amount you can *spend* as opposed to the amount of income you can generate. The former amount will usually be less because you have to pay income tax on most sources of income.

You can find the calculator at **enhancement4.morneaushepell.com**. There is no charge for using it.

The first time you would use the calculator is when you are thinking of retiring and you want to know how much income you could receive starting immediately. If you have already retired, the calculator will still be useful. The calculator always assumes the user

is either retiring immediately or has already retired. It does not calculate income if your retirement isn't expected to happen until some
future year.

It is recommended that you choose a level of retirement income that
is somewhere between the safe income target and the best-estimate
target. While you can use the calculator as frequently as you wish, it
probably makes the most sense to use it on an annual basis or after
an important financial event has occurred, such as receiving an inheritance or a major stock market correction.

When using the calculator to calculate the combined retirement
income range for you and your spouse, make sure you don't double
count. For instance, if you have rental income of $20,000 a year, enter
the amount the same as you would for tax purposes. If it is deemed
to be all your income, then enter $20,000 for yourself and $0 for your
spouse. If it is shared equally, enter $10,000/$10,000.

The assumptions underlying the calculator are given in Table C.1.

Table C.1: Assumptions Used in the Calculations

Income-drawing strategy	It is assumed that assets that are not tax-sheltered will be drawn down first, then income from RRIFs and LIFs and, lastly, from TFSAs as employment income. Rental income, annuities, defined benefit pensions, OAS and CPP are also taken into account.
Future adjustments to income	Total income is assumed to rise in accordance with the spend-ing rate described in Chapter 4. The long-term inflation rate is assumed to be 2.2% a year.
Assets remaining	In calculating the income targets, it is assumed that an amount equal to 10% of the initial assets must be preserved at the time of death.
Asset mix in the RRIF and TFSA	30% in Canadian stocks (S&P/TSX Capped Composite Index), 30% in foreign stocks (MSCI World Index) and 40% in Canadian government bonds (FTSE TMX Canada Universe Bond Index)
Enhancements	In determining income levels, it is assumed that Enhance-ments 2 and 3 will be implemented, meaning the purchase of an annuity at retirement with 30% of RRIF and LIF assets and the deferral of CPP pension until 70, if possible.
Investment fees	Assumed to be 50 basis points.

Amount of CPP pension	Unless a specific amount is input, the maximum CPP pension is based on the actual maximum for the current year.
Amount of OAS pension	100% of the maximum for that year
OAS clawback	Based initially on 2017 levels, whereby 100% of OAS is clawed back when individual income exceeds $119,615. These levels will be adjusted annually.
Interest rate for annuity purchase	2.50%
Type of annuity	Joint and 66.7% survivor annuity for couples, life-only annuity with 5-year guarantee for single retirees
Age of last death in the worst-case scenario	95 if higher current age is under 70; otherwise 98.
Ages of death in the best-estimate scenario	90 for the wife; 87 for the husband if the higher current age is under 65; 92/89 if it is between 65 and 75; 94/91 if it is over 75.
Future investment returns	For safe income target, 5th-percentile returns based on a Monte Carlo simulation. For best-estimate scenario, median returns from the same simulation.
Allowance for spending shocks	Shocks are assumed to be absorbed by a reserve fund set up in retirement by saving 5% of annual income until age 80.

Disclaimers

Like any good actuary should, let me finish this section with a few disclaimers:

1. These results are only as good as the data entered into the Monte Carlo simulation. The simulations are supposed to mirror reality, but the underlying assumptions will never be perfect.

2. The income tax calculations are only an approximation, based on the current income tax rates in Ontario. No attempt is made to calculate the impact of tax loss carryforwards, for example. For future years, all tax credits and income tax brackets are assumed to rise with general inflation.

3. I did not reflect the risk of much higher inflation, as an ageing population strongly suggests it is not likely to occur for a long time to come.

4. While the intention is to maintain this calculation tool indefinitely, Morneau Shepell reserves the right to discontinue it or to stop maintaining it at any time.

ENDNOTES

Chapter 3

1. MacDonald, Bonnie-Jeanne, Lars Osberg and Kevin D. Moore. "How Accurately Does 70% Final Employment Earnings Replacement Measure Retirement Income (In)Adequacy? Introducing the Living Standards Replacement Rate (LSRR)." *ASTIN Bulletin: The Journal of the International Actuarial Association*, 46 (2016): 627–76.

Chapter 4

1. Geoffrey N. Calvert. "Pensions and Survival: The Coming Crisis of Money and Retirement." Maclean-Hunter, 1977.

2. Benjamin Tal. "The Looming Bequest Boom—What Should We Expect?" *In Focus* newsletter. CIBC. June 2016.

3. Axel Börsch-Supan. "Savings and Consumption Patterns of the Elderly—The German Case." *Journal of Population Economics*. University of Mannheim. July 1992.

4. Malcolm Hamilton. "The Financial Circumstances of Elderly Canadians and the Implications for the Design of Canada's Retirement Income System." *The State of Economics in Canada.* 2001.

5. David Domeij and Magnus Johannesson. "Consumption and Health." *The B.E. Journal of Macroeconomics*. Volume 6, Issue 1. 2006.

6. Brancati, Cesira Urzi, Brian Beach, Ben Franklin and Matthew Jones. *Understanding Retirement Journeys—Expectations vs Reality*. International Longevity Centre–UK. November 2015.

7. *Building on Canada's Strong Retirement Readiness*. McKinsey & Company. February 2015.

Chapter 5

1. *Society of Actuaries 2015 Risks and Process of Retirement Survey: Report of Findings*. A US survey conducted on behalf of the Society by Mathew Greenwald & Associates, Inc.

2. Stephen P. Bonnar. *Consumption Patterns of the Elderly*. A thesis submitted to the School of Graduate Studies, McMaster University. Page 82. May 2016.

Chapter 8

1. *Society of Actuaries 2015 Risks and Process of Retirement Survey: Report of Findings*, page 125.

Chapter 10

1. Arnott, Robert D., Jason Hsu and Vitali Kalesnik, "The Surprising Alpha From Malkiel's Monkey and Upside Down Strategies." Research Affiliates. August 2013.

Chapter 17

1. Steve Vernon. *The Next Evolution in Defined Contribution Retirement Plan Design*. Leland Stanford Junior University. September 2013.

2. *Decumulation, The Next Critical Frontier: Improvements for Defined Contribution and Capital Accumulation Plans*. ACPM. March 2017.

INDEX

ACKNOWLEDGEMENTS

This book would never have been written if I didn't happen to attend a presentation last summer given by two highly respected Morneau Shepell actuaries—Nigel Branker and Emily Tryssenaar. They made it clear that deriving the maximum possible income from savings with the least possible risk was far from simple.

While this is not a "corporate book," it wouldn't have been possible without the support and encouragement I received from Morneau Shepell's senior management team and board. In particular, I am grateful to Stephen Liptrap, President and CEO of Morneau Shepell, who freed up my time and gave me the resources I needed to write the book.

Michelle Massie, my wife, kindly put up with me during the many months when I was preoccupied with the writing of the book. And as the marketing professional she is, she offered much helpful advice on the positioning of the message.

Lisa Bjornson and others in the Morneau Shepell Retirement Solutions practice provided data from the Monte Carlo simulations that underlie much of the hard analysis contained in the book.

Malcolm Hamilton, Canada's pension guru for the past 30 years, was generous with his time in helping to frame the basic arguments and acting as a sounding board in the early stages of the writing process.

Bonnie-Jeanne MacDonald, FSA, PhD, was enormously helpful to me. As Senior Fellow at the National Institute on Ageing (NIA) at the Ted Rogers School of Management, Ryerson University, she identified existing academic papers that might be relevant for this book and pointed me in the right direction more times than I can remember.

My son Troy Vettese took time out from his busy PhD program at NYU to delve deeply into the manuscript and offer many constructive comments. A number of friends and family—financial planner Rona Birenbaum, my son Gregory and daughter-in-law, Lu Zhao—helped by reading early versions of some of the chapters and pointing out that they could benefit from a more "human" perspective.

Finally, I am grateful to Karen Milner, Michele Kumara and Lindsay Humphreys for their professionalism in turning a raw manuscript into a book.

ABOUT THE AUTHOR

Frederick Vettese has been the Chief Actuary at Morneau Shepell for 26 years. He has spent most of his career advising large organizations on retirement matters. In recent years, his role has morphed into a more public one, helping to dispel myths about retirement planning. *Retirement Income for Life* is Fred's third book on retirement. In addition, his views are frequently aired at industry conferences, in Canada's national newspapers and on radio. Fred was born in Toronto and lives there still, with his wife, Michelle.

For queries on purchasing multiple copies or about potential speaking engagements, please contact Fred at:

fred.vettese@rogers.com